NO COLD WATER, EITHER

JEAN BODMAN

MICHAEL LANZANO

Heinle & Heinle Publishers
Boston, Massachusetts 02116, U.S.A.

HH

Library of Congress Catalog Card Number: 79-57203

Design by Lee Davidson
Illustrated by Michael Johnston
Cover Design by Janet Sutherland

ISBN 0-8384-3229-8
Printing: 9   Year: 9   1 2 3 4 5

Printed in the United States of America

Contents

PREFACE

OVERVIEW

Chapter

Preface

No Cold Water, Either is the second in a series of three readers designed for the adolescent and adult learner of English as a second or foreign language. The first book in the series, *No Hot Water Tonight,* combines careful structural control and adult content. *No Cold Water, Either* picks up where *No Hot Water Tonight* leaves off. We maintained the same attitudes toward language and language study that we did before; which is to say that we believe: (1) that language is, first and foremost, a vehicle for the communication of the entire range of human thoughts and emotions; and (2) that it is our obligation to represent the English language as it is, not necessarily as some grammarians tell us it should be. All else follows from these premises.

Because *No Cold Water, Either* is written for intermediate-level students, we use a wider range of structures and idiomatic expressions. As in *No Hot Water Tonight,* we are careful to be faithful to the spoken form of the language. We control vocabulary and structure by controlling the length of the passages and the contexts in which they appear. Fortunately, as most native speakers avoid, or use infrequently, those structures which we consider "advanced," we had no difficulty in writing an "intermediate" level text that was completely faithful to "normal" idiomatic usage.

No Cold Water, Either has fifteen chapters. Each chapter contains a reading and various vocabulary and comprehension exercises. In addition, there are cultural notes and coping skills material. The readings concern the lives of the tenants in a building on 88th Street in New York City. Whereas the problems dealt with in *No Hot Water Tonight* were those which a newcomer might face immediately—buying clothes and furniture, for example—*No Cold Water, Either* attempts to deal with problems which, while just as real and immediate, may be less amenable to immediate solution. Such endemic problems include coping with crime, dealing with un/underemployment, racism, and understanding the legal system. Added to this is the ever-present anxiety and strain many immigrants feel when they deal with or interact with the larger American culture. To cope with all these problems successfully is a tall order. And to make matters worse, our characters are, alas, only human. And so they succeed and fail, laugh and curse, and cry just like the rest of us.

In *No Cold Water, Either*, we follow five sets of characters, some of whom you remember from *No Hot Water Tonight*. Mrs. Gold is still with us—now eighty years old—and so is the Torres family. You will recognize the tenement on 88th Street, too. Our characters don't have much money, but they somehow make do and enjoy their lives.

Although this series is urban oriented and was designed with immigrants in mind, *No Hot Water Tonight* has been used all over the world, from Algeria to Yugoslavia and Japan. It has been used as a reader with adult beginners, and as a conversation book with intermediate students. It has even been used with advanced EFL students overseas to provide insights into American society. As we have written *No Cold Water, Either* under the same guiding principles, we expect that you will be able to use it in just as wide a range of circumstances.

In doing all this, we have had the help and support of our friends. Among our professional friends our especial thanks go to Susan Lanzano, Joy Noren, Florence Baskoff, Darlene Larsen, and Anne Kelleran. We would also like to thank Detective John Santamaria of the Jersey City, New Jersey Police Department, Lieutenant A. W. Johnson, Jr., of the Briarcliff Manor, New York Police Department, and Mr. Martin L. Masarech, Assistant Vice President of The Peoples' Westchester Savings Bank. These people patiently explained some of the facts of life to us. We thank them all.

Overview of NO COLD WATER, EITHER

As we stated in the overview of *No Hot Water Tonight,* we are well aware that very few classes are homogeneously grouped. This is especially true of "intermediate" classes which can, and almost always do, include the quiet student whose structures are "correct," and the verbal student who rattles on "incorrectly." These students and many more are all intermediate. In addition, students study English for almost as many reasons as there are students. Therefore, in *No Cold Water, Either* we have a wide range of exercises to appeal to different kinds of students. There are fairly "academic" questions that test comprehension for those students who want or need that kind of work. There are cultural notes that analyze aspects of American society, and we have exercises that look carefully at certain representative idioms, phrases, and expressions. The last section of each chapter is the "how to" section: we call it "The Facts of Life." In it we deal concretely with whatever problems we have raised in the chapter. Because we take it as a given that the teacher together with his or her students is in the best position to know what is required for any given class, we do not prescribe what is to be studied. We offer, instead, a variety of materials from which teachers may choose those that will be most appropriate, interesting, or important to their classes. In each chapter, a motivational section and a vocabulary section precede the reading selection. The reading is then followed by cultural notes, comprehension exercises, vocabulary exercises, and coping skills exercises. At the back of the book you will find a section devoted to supplementary grammar exercises.

THE MOTIVATIONAL SECTION. The teacher may begin the chapter by asking the whole class to consider the questions in the motivational section. However, we prefer to use small groups. The questions on the motivational page need not be asked by the teacher, but can be asked by a student from each group. The first set of questions are for discussion. The second set prepares students for the reading and these questions do not require answers. The intent of the motivational section is to interest students in the general topic of the reading that is to follow. Little class time should be spent on this section.

THE VOCABULARY SECTION. Between the two sets of questions is a list of all new vocabulary words contained in the reading selection. If this section is to be taken up in class, all of the words can be pronounced by the teacher and then repeated by the class. If time is limited (as it is in most classes), the teacher can ask the students if there are any words on the list which they do not know and then deal only with those.

The pronunciation of the words in the list is only the first step in helping the students to become familiar with them. Establishing meaning for the new words is the second important step. In addition to writing this ESL reader, we are ESL teachers, ESL supervisors, and learners of other languages. After all the years of experience we have had in the above capacities, it is still a mystery to us why some vocabulary items are learned on first contact and why other items are learned only after extensive exposure. Nevertheless, for whatever reasons, certain categories of words are more easily retained: for example, those words that the student perceives to be useful or necessary; words that are similar and have similar meanings to vocabulary in the student's native language; and words that the student encounters frequently in the spoken and written languages.

THE READING SECTION. In presenting the reading selection we have varied our methods, all of which have worked well. Here are some guidelines:
Students should always be given a chance to read the selection silently to themselves before any other activities take place. Thereafter, the teacher may:
1. read the selections out loud with natural intonation
2. have the students take the various roles in the book
3. tape the selections and have American friends play the role of characters in the book
4. have the students go directly to the comprehension exercises after reading the selection silently

THE CULTURAL NOTES. We feel that if a person wants to learn the language well, she or he must become familiar with the culture that underlies it. In other words, an understanding of the literal meaning of words is not enough. You have to know if and when it is appropriate to use them. For example, when African students asked a teacher we know about his family, he told them, in the course of conversation, that he had two pretty sisters. This simple expression of brotherly pride was greeted with acute embarrassment by his students. When our friend asked his students why they were embarrassed, they told him that it was not right to talk about sisters "that way." So, this teacher discovered the hard way that in that culture one did not talk "publicly" about the physical attributes of a respectable woman, much less a member of one's own family. In our cultural notes, we try to make just such information clear.

The cultural notes can be read at home or in class. The questions following many of the notes are there to encourage discussion and to help students draw parallels or see differences between their own and American culture.

One more thing. Our cultural notes reflect our experience and concerns. You may disagree with some aspects or our portrayal of American life. But, remember, these notes are there to help orient the student to a new culture. As a teacher you are free to alter or augment them in any way you feel would be helpful.

THE COMPREHENSION EXERCISES. We have four kinds of comprehension exercises: "literal" true-false questions called *Face the Facts,* inference true-false questions called *Read Between the Lines,* and two more difficult exercises, one requiring the finding of supporting details, and the second asking the students to make judgments based on an understanding of the material. Even though we allow students to use translation dictionaries we nevertheless encourage them first to try to read the whole story and get the meanings of the new words from context. Needless to say, experienced ESL teachers know that some students will take this advice while others will insist on immediate translation via a dictionary or classmate. Faced with firmly entrenched learning habits, our advice is, surrender! Let the students use their own learning strategies. If they want to look up all the words, so be it. Gentle encouragement to use alternate strategies can be suggested as the students become more confident of their abilities in this new language called English. Encourage them to read the whole story first, then go back; but if they do not follow this advice and prefer to amass long lists of words in their notebooks, they will soon find they must modify their strategies as the stories get longer and the vocabulary "load" increases.

As a teacher you should not worry if the new vocabulary items are not all learned or retained. Do your best to make the words meaningful and try to show the students that the new words are useful. You will not be able to force learning to take place. Learning will occur at its own time and at its own pace. If the students in your class live in the inner city, they will encounter the words used in this book often. The words that need to be learned will be.

One final word on vocabulary: please don't let yourself be tempted to teach those words that the students know just because the words appear on a list at the beginning of each chapter. If students say they know many of the words, resist the temptation to drag out all those wonderful pictures you spent half the night gathering and go immediately to those they don't know. Most of the time in the class should be spent reading and discussing—not learning interminable lists of vocabulary words.

We have found the following techniques helpful in aiding the student to learn and retain the new vocabulary.

1. The teacher can try to make the new words more meaningful by using them in sentences that relate to the students' personal lives.

Example: *advice*
   Juan is seventeen years old and is tired of listening to his older brothers' *advice*. Remember they had a fight last week.

2. Words will more likely be used in a meaningful manner, however, if the students generate sentences which use the words in different contexts. That is to say, it is not enough for the *teacher* to use the words to be learned (as in #1 above); the *students* must become involved in this exercise. With experience, an ESL teacher will know the unfamiliar words in a given list and be able to anticipate questions by preparing visual materials.

Example: *quite a*
   The teacher can show a picture of a famous building or scene and ask the students to describe the picture using *quite a*. In

response to a picture of the Empire State Building, for example, a student might say, "That's quite a building."

3. If this book is to be used for out-of-class reading, then the teacher can encourage the students to purchase a translation dictionary to help them with meanings of new words and to ask an American friend to help with the pronunciation. One word of caution to the teacher: just because students are able to read words, it should not be assumed that they are familiar with alphabetical order as found in dictionaries. We have often encountered students flipping randomly through dictionaries hoping to find the "m's." Take five minutes of class time early in the semester and ask the students to alphabetize a few words written on file cards. Students who do not do this correctly should be given further help.

These exercises are largely self-explanatory. Inferential thinking is not a matter of opinion. If a writer states that it was black outside, the reader may properly infer that it was nighttime unless some other explanation of the darkness is offered. The inference is based upon something other than opinion: information provided by the text, which is interpreted in light of the reader's world experience. For the inference questions, it might be helpful to discuss what inference is and isn't before assigning these questions for the first time.

As suggested in the beginning of the overview, we strongly recommend that the students be given selective exercises according to their needs and abilities. Do not spend too much time on any one item unless the students show great interest in continuing the discussion.

THE VOCABULARY EXERCISES. In our vocabulary exercises, *Mind Your Words,* we discuss the connotative meanings of selected words, phrases, and idioms that have appeared in the reading. We do not attempt to do the job of the students' dictionary, but, rather, discuss aspects of register, appropriateness, and associated meanings. A word about connotative and denotative meaning. The denotative meaning of a word is what you expect to find in the average dictionary. In short, it is the direct, explicit meaning of a word. The connotation of a word is the idea or ideas associated with or suggested by a word in addition to its explicit or denotative meaning. For example, the denotative meaning of *mother* is female parent. The connotations of the word mother, however, include some of the most emotionally charged associations in the language: love, warmth, tenderness, protectiveness, etc.

Because the items under discussion are defined in terms of the context only and because these exercises tackle many of the "gray areas" of language, we suggest that the students be encouraged to work together in groups.

SUPPLEMENTARY GRAMMAR EXERCISES. Some supplementary grammar exercises are included at the end of the book. They are intended not to give practice in every structure in the book, but instead to reinforce work that may have already taken place in the grammar portion of the class. When the students do not need this added practice, these exercises should not be assigned. These exercises are divided into two parts. The first is called *How It Goes Together* and deals with some cohesive features of English. The second is called *How It Is Used* and consists of grammatical exercises that fall into two categories:

1. those that highlight structures not often taught in traditional ESL grammar classes; and
2. those that are often left for the "advanced" level, but which we discuss because an understanding of these structures is necessary if the students are to comprehend the reading fully.

THE CONTENT OF THE BOOK. As was the case in *No Hot Water Tonight,* we can present our students with aspects of American society not usually included in ESL texts. We do so because our students, as members of this society, will have to deal with these questions on one level or another. Therefore, forewarned is, to some degree, forearmed. But we do not preach and neither do our characters. We present everything for the students' consideration. It goes without saying that most people are not like the characters in a book. It also goes without saying that given our students' concerns, we are not going to spend too much time talking about life in either rural Vermont or Marin County, Los Angeles, as delightful as those places undoubtedly are. If after reading chapters nine or eleven a student asks, "Are most Americans racists?", what do you do? Do you as a teacher affirm or deny? Or say nothing? Our suggestion is to ask the class

to consider what their own experiences have been. We don't think it is possible for any book or any teacher to undertake the job of spokesperson for American society.

It has been our experience that, as a rule, our students are considerably more "conservative," in terms of social change, than their American teachers. Some classes will find certain topics—drug abuse, perhaps—disturbing. If you have such a class, don't dwell on the offending topic. The process of learning English is not served if students actively fear that English is a Trojan horse for a host of unacceptable or threatening values. A class that we know of in the Middle East was not particularly excited about using *No Hot Water Tonight* until they got to the chapters (fourteen through eighteen) where Sally and Emily go to a bar to meet men. This aspect of American life—the fact that it was possible—was so fascinating to them that they spent the rest of the semester on these five chapters. And that's fine with us. That's the way it should be.

In conclusion, we have written the book to appeal to as many levels and as many types of students as possible. The exercises are designed so that students may interact with one another independently of the teacher. It is extremely important that the teacher understand that the value of these readings will in some way be lessened if he/she beats them to death by assigning too many exercises or dwelling too long on vocabulary. We hope that the chapters will be covered rapidly in class and that the students will even be encouraged to read on by themselves if they do not need supervision.

Jean W. Bodman
Michael R. Lanzano

x

ONE ONE ONE ONE ONE ONE

Some questions you might like to discuss with your classmates:

How long have you lived at your present address?
How many different places have you lived in?
The last time you moved, did you move yourself or did you pay someone
  to move your things?

Say these words

after your teacher or after an American friend.

		phrases
blan'·ket	seat	had bet'·ter
for'·ward	slam	keep an eye on
gold'·en	sun'·shine	let's get go'·ing
moan (v.)	sup·pose'	look out for
My (interjection)	ten'·ants	num'·ber one
oc·ca'·sion·al·ly	un·lock'	pull up
re·spect'	warm (v.)	

You may remember Mrs. Gold from NO HOT WATER TONIGHT. In chapter one of this text, Mrs. Gold is in her first floor apartment, looking out the window.

As you read the story, think about these questions:

Who is Mrs. Gold?
What does she see out her window?
Who are the young men?
What are they doing?

LOOKING OUT FOR NUMBER ONE

Mrs. Gold is sitting in her chair near the window. She isn't feeling very well. Her eyes open and close as she rests in the sunshine coming through the window. The sun, like a golden blanket, warms and holds her. Occasionally, some noise makes her open her eyes and look out at 88th Street.

A small truck pulls up in front of the building. Mrs. Gold opens her eyes.

"You can't park there," she says to herself. "People have

no respect for the law these days. No respect at all." Mrs. Gold sits forward in her chair. A young man gets out of the truck, slams the door and walks to the building. Mrs. Gold listens. He unlocks the front door.

"Listen to that," she says to herself. "He must have a key." She hears him walk up the stairs. "I'd better go and keep an eye on things."

She tries to get up, but she sits back down in her chair. "Oh," she moans, "I'm getting old."

She looks at the truck outside. There is another young man in the front seat. On the side of the truck in big red letters are the words: MOVE IT YOURSELF.

The first young man comes down the stairs and goes outside. "Okay, Nate, let's get going." The other one gets out of the truck. Together they open the back and begin taking out some chairs, tables, and a bed.

"Ah," says Mrs. Gold talking to herself again, "they must be the new tenants in 5W. My, they're young. They look like children. I suppose that's what happens when you get old. Everybody looks young. I wonder . . . . Oh well, I'll meet them later."

She closes her eyes and goes to sleep.

CULTURAL NOTES*

1. Forty million Americans move every year. The average American moves once every five years. Only three percent of Americans live in one house all their lives.
   - *How many times have you moved in your life?*
2. It is common for young people who work and are over twenty-one years old to have their own apartments. Both the parents and their children think this is a good idea. These young people move frequently. They usually do not have much money or furniture, so when they move, they usually rent a truck for the day and ask their friends to help them.
3. In Mrs. Gold's building, each floor has two apartments.

The apartments on the *east* side of the building have the letter "E" after the floor number. The apartments on the *west* side of the building have the letter "W". So the new tenants are moving into 5W—the fifth floor, west side. Mrs. Gold lives in 1W.
   - *How are apartments numbered in your building? In your country?*

Cultural notes contain explanations of things in the reading our students didn't know about urban American culture. This is how we explained these issues to them. These facts may not be true for all Americans, but we hope they help foreign students understand our culture a little better.

COMPREHENSION EXERCISES

Face the Facts

If the sentence is true, write "T."
If the sentence is false, write "F."

1. ___ Mrs. Gold is an old lady.

2. ___ It's a sunny day.

3. ___ The young men park their truck in front of the building.

4. ___ Mrs. Gold talks to herself.

5. ___ Mrs. Gold talks to the young men.

Read Between the Lines

If the sentence is true, write "T." If the sentence is false, write "F." Make an inference.

1. ___ The young men are new tenants in the building.

2. ___ One of the young men has a key to the front door.

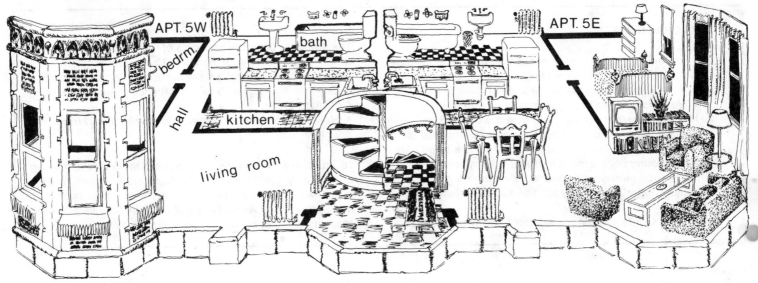

3. ___ It's illegal to park in front of the building.

4. ___ Mrs. Gold does not want to meet the young men.

5. ___ The new tenants are children.

MORE DIFFICULT COMPREHENSION EXERCISES
Find the Supporting Details

Mrs. Gold says, "They must be the new tenants in 5W."
She sees and hears three things that lead her to this
conclusion. See how many you can find:

1.

2.

3.

Make a Judgment

Mrs. Gold gives the following opinion:
   "People have no respect for the law these days."
Do you think this is true? Discuss your answer and your
reasons for it with the students in your class.

VOCABULARY EXERCISES

Mind Your Words

occasionally
respect
suppose
my

keep an eye on

Look at the following exercises. They will help you understand how the items are used. You may use your dictionary to find their definitions. Remember, we are working with the meanings of the items as they appear in the story; they may have other meanings in other contexts.

OCCASIONALLY

"*Occasionally,* some noise makes her open her eyes and look out at 88th Street."

Answer the following questions:

1. Is Mrs. Gold watching 88th Street carefully? *No*
2. What do you think—are her eyes open most of the time?

Look at the following statements. Decide which of them are true for you and correct to say in English. Be prepared to explain your decisions.

1. The sun rises occasionally. *No*
2. I think about my grandparents occasionally. *c*
3. I eat hamburgers occasionally.
4. I get married occasionally. *∼*

RESPECT

"People have no *respect* for the law these days. No respect at all."

Decide which of these sentences are true for you and correct to say in English. Be prepared to explain your decisions.

1. I respect the law. *c*
2. I respect the soup. *×*
3. I respect my family.
4. I respect the President of the U.S.
5. I respect my vacation.
6. I respect the power of the ocean. *c*
7. I respect my friend's intelligence. *c*
8. I respect my friend's face.

SUPPOSE

"I *suppose* that's what happens when you get old."

Choose synonyms for *suppose* as it is used in the sentence above. More than one synonym may be possible.

1. imagine *∼*   *similar*
2. know *×*
3. think *∼*
4. am sure *×*
5. hope *×*
6. guess *✓*

Choose the sentences that are correct in English under normal circumstances. Be prepared to explain your decisions.

1. I suppose I have three children. ✗
2. I suppose I'll take a vacation this summer.
3. Do you suppose Willie is happy?
4. I suppose today is her birthday. *you have reason*
5. Do you suppose you are from your country?

MY
"*My*, they're young."

In the sentence above, Mrs. Gold says "*my*" to show that she is:
1. angry
2. unhappy
3. a little surprised
4. very happy
5. very surprised

Which sentences are correct in English under normal circumstances? Be prepared to explain your decisions.
1. My, our plane is on fire. ✗
2. My, I got fired.
3. My, I got four letters today.
4. My, there's a body on the roof. *dead body*
5. My, what a cold day.

As used above, my *is an interjection. It is used most often by women. Men use it less often.*

KEEP AN EYE ON
"I'd better go and *keep an eye on* things."

Choose the appropriate synonyms for *keep an eye on* as it is used in the sentence above. More than one synonym may be possible.
1. pay attention to
2. watch
3. forget
4. buy
5. see

Usually, you keep an eye on *something when you expect that something bad, dangerous, or harmful may happen. You might also* keep an eye on *something or someone that you want to protect.*

Choose the sentences that are correct in English under normal circumstances. Be prepared to explain your decisions.
1. The tourist is keeping an eye on the pyramids. ✗ *absorb*
2. My neighbor is keeping an eye on our apartment while we are away.
3. When I get up in the morning, I keep an eye on my apartment.
4. The U.S.S.R. is keeping an eye on China.
5. Keep an eye on the baby, please. *watch*
6. I'm keeping an eye on television tonight.

Think about this one twice before you answer:

7. The baby is keeping an eye on his mother so his mother won't get hurt.

THE FACTS OF LIFE

The Phone Book

When you move, you have to decide if you want to move yourself or if you want to use a moving company. In order to make this decision, you may want to call a number of companies and get the following information:

1. How much does it cost to hire a moving company?
2. Do you have to make a reservation with them a long time in advance?
3. What will they do for you?

When you have these answers, you can decide whether or not you want to use a moving company. Ask yourself these questions:

1. Do I have enough money to pay for a moving company?
2. Do I have any furniture that I can't move myself?
3. Do I have any friends who could help me move?
4. Do I have a lot of time to move or must I do it in one day?
5. If I need several days, can I move my things into the new place ahead of time? Would I have to pay additional rent?
6. Should I sell my old furniture and buy new things? Would this save me money?

After thinking about these questions, you might want to go to the phone book and call other companies to get further information.

There are usually two different places to find information: the white pages and the yellow pages. The white pages list people and companies alphabetically by name. The yellow pages list people and companies by what they do. If you want to move yourself, look in the yellow pages under:

Rentals—Truck Renting and Leasing.

Rentals—Trailer Renting and Leasing.

The next time you think about moving, you might want to call several truck rental companies and ask them the following:

1. What size trucks do you have?
   (Tell them how many rooms you have to move.)
   How large a truck will I need?
2. How much do the different trucks cost to rent for one day? for two days? etc. Do I have to buy insurance?
3. Do you want a deposit? How much?
4. Do you accept checks, credit cards, a money order, or only cash? What kind of identification do you want?
5. Do I need a special drivers' license?
6. Is gas included?
7. Do you rent furniture pads, hand trucks, etc.? How much?
8. Do you sell boxes?
9. How far in advance do I have to reserve the truck?
10. Do I have to return the truck to the same place? How much extra does it cost to return the truck to another place?

Do insurance included in that price?

EXERCISES

1. If you would like to have practice in speaking and understanding English on the phone, try this activity now.

   Look in the phone book and find a few moving companies or truck rental companies. One student can call each company. Choose questions from the list above. Compare the answers received. Which company has the best deal?

2. You might also like to share past experiences and information about moving with your classmates.

See supplementary exercises on pages 147 and 158.

Some questions you might like to discuss with your classmates:

Did you ever have to report a fire or a crime?

What did you do?

Did the police or firemen come quickly?

What happened?

Say these words

after your teacher or after an American friend.

buz'·zer
con·nect'
door'·bell
just
lo'·cate
op'·er·a·tor

pale
re·port'
roof
shape
top (adj.)

slang
wast'·ed

phrases
go a·head'
pa·trol' car
take a look

In chapter two, Willie, the new tenant in 5W, knocks on Mrs. Gold's door.

As you read the story, think about these questions:

Why does Willie Dorio go to Mrs. Gold's apartment?
Who(m) does he call?
What did he see on the roof?
Who are O'Neill and Walters?

WASTED

(There's a knock on Mrs. Gold's door.)

Mrs. Gold: Who is it?

Willie Dorio: Willie Dorio. I live on the top floor.

Mrs. Gold: *(opening the door)* Come in. I'm Mrs. Gold. I saw you move in the other day. What can I do for you?

Willie Dorio: Can I use your phone? I don't have one yet. They said they would connect my phone today, but they didn't. I just moved in this week.

Mrs. Gold: I know. Well, it's no trouble. The phone's over there.

Willie: I was on the roof just now, and . . . and uh . . . .

Mrs. Gold: Sit down, Mr. Dorio.

Willie: Willie.

Mrs. Gold: Willie. You look pale. Are you all right?

Willie: Yes, I'm all right, thanks. I was on the roof just now and . . . listen, I'd better use your phone now.

Mrs. Gold: Certainly, go ahead.

(Willie dials the police emergency number.)

Police: Operator 210. Is this an emergency?

Willie: Yes. I want to report a person on the roof. I think he's dead.

Mrs. Gold: What? Dead?

Police: What's your name?

Willie: William Dorio.

Police: Where are you located?

Willie: 229 88th Street. I'm in apartment 1W, but the body is on the roof.

Police: What number are you calling from?

Willie: Let me see. *(Willie looks at the number on the phone.)* 555-7720.

Police: Did you find the body?

Willie: I guess so.

Police: Please wait there. We'll send a patrol car immediately.

(Willie hangs up the phone.)

Mrs. Gold: A body? On our roof? Terrible. How terrible! Willie, why don't you sit down? You don't look so good. Sit down, Willie.

Willie: I'm all right, thanks.

Mrs. Gold: Of course you are. Tell me what happened.

Willie: I was on the roof just now and I saw this dark shape in the corner. I went nearer and saw it was a person. A young guy. He didn't move.

(The doorbell rings. Mrs. Gold gets up and goes to the door.)

Mrs. Gold: Think of it. On *our* roof!

(She presses the buzzer and speaks through the intercom.)

Mrs. Gold: Who is it?

Policeman: Police.

(She presses the buzzer to let them in the front door and opens her door.)

Mrs. Gold: Oh, yes. That was fast. I'm Mrs. Gold.

Policeman: Did you report the body on the roof?

Willie: No. *I* did.

Policeman: I'm Officer O'Neill and this is Officer Walters. Let's take a look. Come with us, please.

(The policemen and Willie go up to the roof. A few minutes

later they return. Walters goes to the patrol car. O'Neill knocks on Mrs. Gold's door.)

Mrs. Gold: Who is it?
Policeman: Officer O'Neill.

(Mrs. Gold opens the door.)

Mrs. Gold: Well, is he dead?

COMPREHENSION EXERCISES

Face the Facts

If the sentence is true, write "T." If the sentence is false, write "F."

1. ___ Mrs. Gold has a phone in her apartment.

2. ___ Willie moved into the building several months ago.

3. ___ Willie calls the fire department.

4. ___ Willie goes to the roof with the policemen.

5. ___ Willie tells Mrs. Gold what he saw on the roof.

Read Between the Lines

If the sentence is true, write "T." If the sentence is false, write "F." Make an inference.

1. ___ Willie is pale because he's very upset about what he saw.

2. ___ The policemen arrive soon after Willie calls.

3. ___ At the *end* of this story, Willie doesn't know if the young man is dead or not.

4. ___ At the *end* of this story, Mrs. Gold doesn't know if the young man is dead or not.

5. ___ When the police say to Willie, "Come with us, please," they are making a polite request.

MORE DIFFICULT COMPREHENSION EXERCISES

Find the Supporting Details

Willie says about the young man, "I think he's dead." Several things probably led him to this conclusion. See how many you can list:

1.

2.

3.

Make a Judgment

There are deaths every day in New York City. Do you think Mrs. Gold should be so surprised by the body on the roof? Why or why not? Discuss your opinion and your reasons for it with your classmates.

VOCABULARY EXERCISES

Mind Your Words

top
connect
pale

Look at the following exercises. They will help you understand how these words are used. You may use your dictionary to find their definitions. Remember, we are working with the meanings of the words as they appear in the dialogue; they may have other meanings in other contexts.

TOP
"I live on the *top* floor."

In this context, *top* refers to:
1. quality
2. size
3. location
4. importance

If you live on the *top* floor of your building, the building probably has:
1. one floor
2. two floors or more

Choose the best synonym for *top* as it is used in the story:
1. best
2. highest
3. most expensive

CONNECT
"They said they would *connect* my phone today."

Which of these words are synonyms for *connect* as it is used in the sentence above? More than one synonym may be possible.
1. install
2. put in
3. marry
4. remove
5. join

Which of these sentences use *connect* correctly?
1. You have to *connect* the TV before it will work.
2. I *connected* the soy sauce and the chicken.
3. Did the man *connect* your new air conditioner?
4. He *connected* his money in the bank.

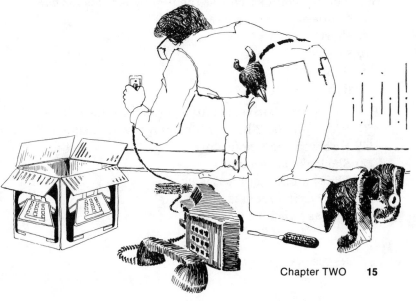

PALE

"You look *pale*."

In the sentence above, *pale* has a:

1. positive meaning
2. negative meaning
3. neutral meaning

Choose one:
Pale refers to:
1. size
2. shape
3. color

Based on the context, choose the best synonyms for *pale*:
1. colorless
2. short
3. sick
4. thin
5. light

Pale can have positive, negative, or netural meanings in different contexts. Which of the following are negative?
1. He's wearing a *pale* shirt.
2. She looks *pale* today.
3. That hamburger meat is *pale*.
4. Their living room is *pale* blue.
5. He has *pale* blue eyes.

Which of the following can be *pale*?
1. people
2. the color of a house
3. the snow
4. the sky
5. hair
6. teeth

Can a sick person look *pale?*
Can a healthy person look *pale?*

THE FACTS OF LIFE

Emergencies

Emergencies are facts of life. Many emergencies require the help of either the police department or the fire department.

Both the police department and the fire department have emergency telephone numbers that you can call any hour of the day or night. If you dial "0", the telephone operator will connect you with the correct emergency number. All you have to say is, "Operator, this is an emergency. Give me the police (or fire) department."

You can save time if you know the correct number.

People at the fire department say, when you have an emergency, remember two things:
KEEP CALM, and
KEEP SPEAKING ENGLISH.

EXERCISES

1. Find out the telephone numbers of the police station and fire station in your neighborhood.

   POLICE: _____

   FIRE: _____

You might also want to know the following numbers, especially if you have children:

FAMILY DOCTOR: _____

POISON CONTROL: _____

The telephone company suggests that you keep these numbers on or next to your phone.

2. Look back at the story and Willie's emergency call. The police operator wants to know six things. Write down as many as you can find. Here are two to help you get started:

  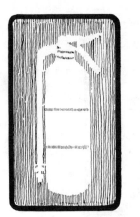 

FLAMMABLE

    1. Is it an emergency?

    2. What's the problem?

3. Have you ever reported a crime or a complaint to the police? What happened? Share your experiences, if you wish, with your classmates.

4. Get together with another student. One student will report an emergency; the other student will receive the call. Practice a few of the following situations, or make some up yourself.

    1. A child just swallowed a whole bottle of vitamins. Call the doctor or poison control.

    2. There's smoke coming from the wall in your kitchen. Call the fire department or the operator.

    3. Your friend has a fever. You take his/her temperature. It's 104° F.
    Call the doctor or an ambulance.

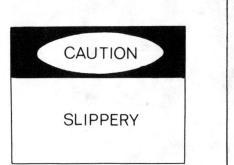

CAUTION

SLIPPERY

RADIATION

KEEP AWAY

See supplementary exercises on pages 148 and 159.

THREE EE THREETHREE

Some questions you might like to discuss with your classmates:

Have you ever found someone you thought was dead?
What did you do?
How did you feel?
In the last chapter, Mrs. Gold's last words are, "Is he dead?" What do you think?

Say these words

after your teacher or after an American friend.

ap·pre'·ci·ate	rou·tine'	*phrases*
case	scene	D.A.'s Of'·fice
co·op·er·a'·tion	state'·ment	dead ring'·er
de·tec'·tive	sta'·tion	get back to
en'·ter	thin	Me'·di·cal Ex·am'·in·er's
i·den'·ti·fy	touch	Of'·fice
in'·no·cent	turn	
make	weigh	

In this chapter, Willie is questioned by the police.

As you read the story, think about these questions:

Why does the policeman ask so many questions?
Who does Willie look like?
Does Mrs. Gold recognize the young man?
What does Willie have to do at the end of the story?
Do you think Willie is telling the truth?

A DEAD RINGER

Mrs. Gold: Is he dead?

(Officer O'Neill enters Mrs. Gold's apartment with Willie. He turns and speaks to Mrs. Gold.)

O'Neill: How did you know it was a man?
Mrs. Gold: Willie told me.
O'Neill: I see. Yeah, he's dead.
             (O'Neill turns to Willie)
             Okay. I'd like to ask you a few questions.
Willie: All right.
O'Neill: What's your full name?
Willie: William Dorio.
O'Neill: *(writing in his notebook)* D-O-R-I-O?
Willie: Yes.
O'Neill: Your address?
Willie: 229 88th Street. Apartment 5W.
O'Neill: You don't live in this apartment?

Willie: No. I live upstairs. I came to use Mrs. Gold's phone. Nobody else was home.
O'Neill: Why didn't you use *your* phone?
Willie: I don't have one yet. I just moved in. Hey . . . what is this?
O'Neill: I'm just getting the facts for our report. When did you find the body?
Willie: I guess it was about 8:00.
O'Neill: Did you touch anything up there before we came?
Willie: No. When he didn't move, I came down here to call.
O'Neill: Did you know the guy?
Willie: No.
O'Neill: Have you ever seen him before?
Willie: No.
O'Neill: Are you sure?
Willie: Yes! I'm sure.
O'Neill: What was he doing on the roof?
Willie: I don't know. How am I supposed to know?
O'Neill: Take it easy. I'm just asking. Did you take anything away from the scene?
Willie: No!
O'Neill: Okay. Let's get back to you. How old are you?
Willie: Twenty-one.

(O'Neill looks at Willie carefully.)

O'Neill: Are you sure?

Willie:	Of course. You think I don't know how old I am?
O'Neill:	Do you work?
Willie:	Yes.
O'Neill:	Where?
Willie:	"Pretty Feet." It's a shoe store on 3rd Avenue and 80th Street. I'm a salesman. Why are you asking me all these questions?
O'Neill:	It's just routine. What were you doing up on the roof?
Willie:	I like to go up there.
O'Neill:	Why?

Willie:	I like it.
O'Neill:	At night?
Willie:	Sure.

(Officer Walters returns.)

Walters:	*(to Officer O'Neill)* The people from the Medical Examiner's office and the D.A.'s office just went up there.
Mrs. Gold:	Officer?
Walters:	Yes, ma'am?
Mrs. Gold:	How did he die?

Walters: We don't know yet.

Mrs. Gold: What did he look like? Maybe I know him. I know everyone on the block.

Walters: He's white, male, about 5'9", thin—about 135—black hair, about twenty years old, a good-looking kid.

Mrs. Gold: Why, that sounds like you, Willie!

Willie: I weigh a lot more than 135.

Walters: He had no identification on him.

(He turns to Mrs. Gold.)

Would you like to try to identify the body? We'd appreciate it.

Mrs. Gold: I'm always glad to help.

Walters: I think they're bringing it down now.

(He looks out into the hall and sees the men bringing the body down the stairs.)

Yes. Take a look, Mrs. Gold.

(Mrs. Gold looks at the young man.)

Mrs. Gold: He's so young. So young.

O'Neill: Do you know him?

Mrs. Gold: So quiet and innocent.

O'Neill: Mrs. Gold! Do you know him?

Mrs. Gold: Hmmm? Oh, no. I've never seen him before. Willie, he looks like you. He could be your brother.

Willie: I don't have a brother.

Mrs. Gold: I didn't mean he *was* your brother. But he could be.

Willie: Listen. I'm going upstairs.

Walters: Can you come down to the station to make a statement and speak to the detectives on the case?

Willie: Now?

O'Neill: Yes.

Willie: Do I have to?

O'Neill: Yes. We'll drive you over.

(to Mrs. Gold)

Thank you for your cooperation. Sorry to trouble you.

CULTURAL NOTES

1. Almost everyone in the U.S. has at least one phone in his apartment or house. It is considered a necessity.
   - *Do you feel that you have to have a phone?*
2. In the U.S. when someone dies in an unusual way, the Medical Examiner is called. The Medical Examiner must look at the body where it was found and fill out a report.
3. The D.A. is the District Attorney. When the police investigate a complaint, they present the information to the D.A. The D.A. is a lawyer who represents the state at trials. There is usually one D.A.'s office in each county.
4. In the story, two kinds of policemen are mentioned—patrolmen (officers) and detectives (sergeants). Patrolmen usually investigate complaints first and detectives take over if the crime is serious.

for Pretty Feet

1. ___ The young man on the roof is Willie's brother.

2. ___ Willie said he knew the young man.

3. ___ Willie is a shoe salesman.

4. ___ Mrs. Gold identified the young man.

5. ___ The policemen are going to drive Willie to the police station.

Read Between the Lines

If the sentence is true, write "T." If the statement is false, write "F." Make an inference.

1. ___ The police believe that Willie is telling the truth.

2. ___ The police think it is unusual that Willie doesn't have a phone.

3. ___ A lot of people go up on their apartment roofs at night.

4. ___ Willie is good-looking.

5. ___ Walters and O'Neill are police detectives.

COMPREHENSION EXERCISES

Face the Facts

If the sentence is true, write "T." If the sentence is false, write "F."

MORE DIFFICULT COMPREHENSION EXERCISES

Find the Supporting Details

The policeman says, "I'm just getting the facts for our report." Pretend you are the policeman and fill in the following information.

1. Name of complainant _____

2. Address of complainant _____

3. Name of victim _____

Make a Judgment

Read the story again. Look at how Willie and the policemen react to each other. How does Willie feel when the policeman asks him all the questions? Does O'Neill become more or less sympathetic to Willie by the end of the story? Would you act differently? Discuss these questions with your classmates.

VOCABULARY EXERCISES

Mind Your Words

case
thin
male

Look at the following exercises. They will help you understand how these words are used. You may use your dictionary to find their definitions. Remember, we are working with the meanings of the words as they appear in the dialogue; they may have other meanings in other contexts.

CASE

"Can you come down to the station to make a statement and speak to the detectives on the *case*?"

Choose the best synonym for *case* in this context:
1. piece of furniture
2. box
3. investigation

Judges, lawyers, doctors, and policemen work on "cases." Which of the following work on cases, too?
1. musicians
2. social workers
3. truck drivers
4. detectives
5. psychiatrists

THIN

"He's white, male, about 5'9", *thin*—about 135—black hair, about twenty years old, a good-looking kid."

In this context, the word *thin* describes:
1. weight
2. height
3. color

In the United States, most people want to be thin, and think it is a compliment to be called thin. Therefore, in the U.S., *thin* is usually part of a:
1. positive description
2. negative description
3. neutral description

MALE

"He's white, *male*, about 5'9", thin—about 135—black hair, about twenty years old, a good-looking kid."

The description above was given by a policeman. It is *not* supposed to be:
1. technical
2. romantic
3. accurate
4. funny

A woman describing her handsome boyfriend would usually call him:
1. a good-looking man
2. a good-looking male

THE FACTS OF LIFE

Ordering a Telephone

It's quite easy to get a phone in the U.S. if you have some money. First, you must find out where the telephone business office is. Look in the phone book for *Business Offices* on page 1 or page 2.

If you are interested, find and write the address of the nearest telephone business office in your town here:

_____

If you want a phone, you will have to go to the Business Office and order one. Here are some of the things they will want to know:

Name _____

Employer _____

Employer's address _____

Employer's telephone number _____

Position at work _____

Supervisor's name _____

Length of time on the job _____

Number of people who will use the phone _____

Their relationship _____

Spouse's name _____

Prior service (number) _____

If no prior service, why? _____

Destination of most calls made _____

Volume of calls _____

After you fill this out, the clerk will ask you for a deposit. The usual deposit is about $50.00. If they think you will be making a lot of long-distance calls, they ask for a bigger deposit. The telephone company will keep the deposit for about a year. Then they will return it to you with six percent interest. If you have had a phone in the U.S. before (in *your* name) and you paid your bills, you may not have to give a deposit.

Phones come in many styles and colors, and they have different costs.

You have to pay a fee to rent the phone and to have service each month. The fee is not the same in all towns and cities.

One friend in New Jersey has two white phones and he pays $8.66 a month.

Another friend in New York has two black phones and she pays $11.66 a month.

So you can see that it's cheaper to have a phone in New Jersey than in New York.

For the money you pay each month, you receive:
1. calls from other people to you
2. a certain number of free calls
3. your name in the phone book
4. a phone book

You have to pay extra for:

1. long-distance calls
2. extra local calls
3. more than one name in the phone book
4. *not* putting your name in the phone book (an unlisted number)

The phone company will ask you how you want your name listed. Many people do not put their full names in the phone book. Sometimes crazy people call women and bother them. Some women use just their initials so strangers can't tell if they are men or women.

Name	Phone Book
Jean W. Bodman	Bodman, J. W.
Michael R. Lanzano	Lanzano, M. R.

After you order your phone and pay a deposit, you make an appointment to have your phone installed. Usually you can have your phone in a few days.

OPTIONAL EXERCISE

Here is an exercise that you might like to do:

Use the form on page 26. One student will ask questions. Another student will answer them. Think about your answers so you will not have to give a larger deposit than necessary.

See supplementary exercises on pages 148 and 161.

Some questions you might like to discuss with your classmates:

How do you feel about the police?

Do you like them? Do you trust them?

Do you feel that they do a good job in your neighborhood?

after your teacher or after an American friend.

dis·like′ (v.)	stuff (n., *slang*)	go through the wring′·er
ex·act′·ly	thou′·sand	it pays + *infinitive*
mur′·der		keep *(possessive)* mouth shut
mur′·der·er	*phrases*	Keep your nose clean.
nee′·dle	be made	kick *(someone)* out
o′·ver·dose	be on drugs	mind *(possessive)* (own) busi′·ness
ques′·tion (v.)	good guy	slip *(someone something)*
sign (v.)		type *(something)* up

In this chapter, the police continue the investigation.

As you read the story, think about these questions:

What happened to Willie at the police station?
How does Willie think the boy died?
How do the police think the boy died?
What did the police want to know about Willie?
What were the police looking for around the building?
Does Willie know more than he is telling?

THROUGH THE WRINGER

(The next day. Mrs. Gold is sitting at her window and sees Willie coming home from work.)

Mrs. Gold: Hello, Willie, how are you today? How did it go last night at the police station?

Willie: I told them exactly what I saw and did on the roof. Somebody typed it up and I signed it. The last thing O'Neill said to me was, "Keep your nose clean, kid."

Mrs. Gold: I made a cake this afternoon. Come in and have a cup of coffee.

Willie: Sure. Why not? I don't feel like going up on the roof tonight.

Mrs. Gold: I'm not surprised.

(Mrs. Gold gets up and opens the door for Willie. Willie goes into Mrs. Gold's apartment. She looks closely at Willie's face.)

Willie: What's the matter? Is my face dirty?

Mrs. Gold: No, it's not dirty. Willie, how old are you, really?

Willie: Eighteen. But don't tell anyone. They'll kick me out.

Mrs. Gold: I won't. Excuse me for a minute, and I'll get the coffee and cake.

Willie: Can I help?

Mrs. Gold: No. It's all made. Come into the kitchen.

(They go into the kitchen.)

Mrs. Gold: Sit down.

Willie: I need a cup of coffee. I really feel sorry for that guy.

Mrs. Gold: What guy?

Willie: The kid on the roof.

Mrs. Gold: Did you know him?

Willie: No. I never saw him before. But I really feel sorry for him.

Mrs. Gold: Why?

Willie: He had nothing but drugs.

Mrs. Gold: How do you know?

Willie: How else can you die on a roof?

Mrs. Gold: Murder.

Willie: No. Who would want to kill a young kid like him? He died of an overdose.

Mrs. Gold: The police aren't so sure.

Willie: What do you mean?

Mrs. Gold: They were here all afternoon. They questioned everybody on the block.

Willie:	Who is "they?" O'Neill and Walters?		Willie:	I wonder why.
Mrs. Gold:	No. Some detectives.		Mrs. Gold:	I think they wanted to find out if you knew the dead boy.
Willie:	What did they want?			
Mrs. Gold:	They asked a lot of questions about you.		Willie:	I told them a thousand times I didn't.
Willie:	Yeah? Like what?		Mrs. Gold:	I'm sure it's just routine. Oh, yes . . . and they wanted to know if you ever acted strangely.
Mrs. Gold:	They wanted to know how long you've been living here, and . . .			

Willie: Who is "they?" O'Neill and Walters?
Mrs. Gold: No. Some detectives.
Willie: What did they want?
Mrs. Gold: They asked a lot of questions about you.
Willie: Yeah? Like what?
Mrs. Gold: They wanted to know how long you've been living here, and . . .
Willie: I told them how long I've been living here.
Mrs. Gold: . . . what kind of person you are, and who your friends are, and . . . .
Willie: I don't believe it! What else did they want to know?
Mrs. Gold: Uh . . . what kind of people went in and out of your apartment. And they wanted to know if you knew anyone from the neighborhood.

Willie: I wonder why.
Mrs. Gold: I think they wanted to find out if you knew the dead boy.
Willie: I told them a thousand times I didn't.
Mrs. Gold: I'm sure it's just routine. Oh, yes . . . and they wanted to know if you ever acted strangely.
Willie: They're trying to find out if I'm on drugs. Look, maybe somebody slipped him some bad stuff. But it wasn't me.
Mrs. Gold: I believe you, Willie. I told the police what a nice young man you were.
Willie: Thanks.
Mrs. Gold: Willie? Did you see a needle on the roof?
Willie: No. It was dark up there. But they asked me that, too.

Mrs. Gold: They were looking for one all around the building.

Willie: There was no needle?

Mrs. Gold: I guess not. Willie—you don't dislike me for talking to the detectives, do you? What else could I do?

Willie: Nothing, I guess. You see! It doesn't pay to be a good guy. I should have kept my mouth shut and not reported that guy on the roof. I should learn to mind my own business.

Mrs. Gold: That's not true, Willie.

Willie: Yes, it is. Now they think I'm a murderer.

CULTURAL NOTES

1. When we invite someone into our homes, we usually offer something to drink, and if we have cake or snacks, we'll put that out, too. We usually only ask a person once if he wants something to eat. If he says "no," we often do not offer again. It is always possible to say later, "I've changed my mind. I think I would like some coffee."

   With food, Americans often put it on the table and say, "Help yourself." We mean exactly what we say. You are supposed to take as much or as little as you want.

   • *What's the custom in your country? Is it different?*

2. When we visit someone's house for an informal dinner, we often ask if we can help. We ask if we can help serve the food, carry plates to the kitchen after dinner, help with the dishes, etc. If our friends do not want help, they will say, "No thanks. Relax and enjoy yourself." These days, both men and women will offer to help. But usually, women will do it first.

   • *Do you think you would ever offer to help?*

3. A serious problem in the U.S. today is drugs. Hard drugs (like heroin, cocaine, LSD, etc.) are illegal without a prescription. Soft drugs (like marijuana, alcohol, tranquilizers, etc.) are sometimes illegal, sometimes not. Americans take a lot of drugs like aspirin, cold tablets, and tranquilizers. We also drink a lot of alcohol, coffee, and tea, which, some people forget, are drugs, too.

COMPREHENSION EXERCISES

Face the Facts

If the sentence is true, write "T." If the sentence is false, write "F."

1. ___ Willie signed his report at the police station.

2. ___ Willie is twenty-one.

3. ___ The police questioned Mrs. Gold about Willie.

4. ___ The police were looking for a needle.

5. ___ Willie is sorry he reported the body on the roof.

Read Between the Lines

If the sentence is true, write "T." If the sentence is false, write "F." Make an inference.

1. ___ Willie felt that things went well at the police station.

2. ___ There is something wrong with renting an apartment at age eighteen.

3. ___ Willie is happy that the police are asking everyone questions about him.

4. ___ Mrs. Gold believes what Willie tells her.

5. ___ Willie is surprised that there was no needle on the roof.

MORE DIFFICULT COMPREHENSION EXERCISES

Find the Supporting Details

1. At first, Willie doesn't believe the boy was murdered. What reason did he give for this?
2. Willie says, "Now they think I'm a murderer." What led him to that conclusion?

Make a Judgment

Based on the information that you have now, how do you think the boy died? Do you think Willie knows more than he is telling? Do you think Willie was responsible in some way for the boy's death?

VOCABULARY EXERCISES
Mind Your Words

murder
stuff

It pays to _____

Look at the following exercises. They will help you understand how these items are used. You may use your dictionary to find their definitions. Remember, we are working with the meanings of the items as they appear in the dialogue. They may have other meanings in other contexts.

MURDER
Willie: How else can you die on a roof?
Mrs. Gold: Murder.

1. In this sentence, *murder* is:
   a. a kind of roof
   b. a way to die
   c. a kind of gun

2. Look up the word *killing* in your dictionary. Compare it with the word *murder*. Use the correct word in the following sentences.
   a. He went to jail for _____ .
   b. There was a lot of _____ during World War II.

Explain to the class why you chose the word that you did for each sentence.

STUFF
"Maybe someone slipped him some bad *stuff*."

1. In this sentence from the dialogue, *stuff* means:
   a. things
   b. food
   c. drugs
   d. medicine

Stuff *is an informal word. It is always singular and you can substitute* stuff *for nonliving mass nouns or plural nouns.*

2. Which of the following items can be called *stuff*?
   a. food
   b. a watch
   c. clothing
   d. things
   e. Mrs. Gold

3. In the sentence, "Where'd I put all the stuff for dinner?" *stuff* has a:
   a. positive meaning
   b. negative meaning
   c. neutral meaning

4. In these two lines, "Look at all the stuff in this apartment! How will we ever move?" *stuff* has a:
   a. positive meaning
   b. negative meaning
   c. neutral meaning

IT PAYS TO . . .
"*It* doesn't *pay to* be a good guy."

1. In the sentence above, Willie is saying that:
   a. he didn't get any money from the police
   b. the police didn't like what he did
   c. he got into trouble for trying to do the right thing

2. "It doesn't pay to be a good guy" is a(n):
   a. happy thing to say
   b. optimistic thing to say
   c. cynical thing to say

THE FACTS OF LIFE

Police Reports

The police will ask you to fill out a report to make a statement if one of the following things happens:
   a. if you report a crime
   b. if you ask to have someone arrested
   c. if you have an automobile accident in which a per-

When you make a statement, the police will probably ask you several questions. They may ask you the same questions more than once. They do this because they want to make sure you are telling the truth, and because sometimes when they ask you the same question more than once, you might remember something more.

The detective will then ask you the questions again and write down your answers. Then, he'll read your answers back to you. Then he'll ask you to swear that your statement is true, and he'll ask you to sign it.

OPTIONAL EXERCISES

You might like to do some of these exercises:
1. Pick one member of the class to go to the local police station to get copies of an automobile accident report. Read it in class and discuss it.
2. Pick another member of the class to go to the police station to get copies of the form for a statement. Read it and discuss it.
3. Call the police in your community. Ask if they have a Community Relations Department. Ask if they can have someone come to your class to talk about the law.

See supplementary exercises on pages 149 and 161.

son is hurt or if the accident involves more than $200.00 damage
d. if something is stolen from you
e. if you see a crime and you are an important witness

Some questions you might like to discuss with your classmates:

Do you know most of the people who live on your block?

How many people can you recognize who live around your neighborhood?

How do you feel about the schools in your area? What do people say about them?

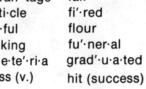

after your teacher or after an American friend.

ac'·tu·al·ly	ed·u·ca'·tion	mo'·ney	shoe
ad·van'·tage	fall	news'·pa·per	won'·der
ar'·ti·cle	fi'·red	pound	
aw'·ful	flour	pub'·lic	
ba'·king	fu'·ner·al	rea'·son	
caf·e·te'·ri·a	grad'·u·a·ted	right (just)	
dress (v.)	hit (success)	sal'·a·ry	

phrases

a·bout' time	call me (*name*)	hard stuff	tell the truth
as e'·ver	down and out	high school	up and com'·ing
be·lieve' in	For good'·ness sake.	on (*possessive*) way	You ne'·ver know.
be out of	fu'·ner·al home	Pleased to meet you.	

*In this chapter Mrs. Gold gets to know Mrs. Fielding
(apartment 3W) better. They talk about neighborhood
news and Mrs. Fielding's children.*

As you read the story, think about these questions:

Who is Henry diBernardo?

What does Mrs. Fielding think of him?

Why don't the Fieldings want Amanda to go to McKinley
  High School?

What do they want for their girls?

What does Mrs. Fielding do for Mrs. Gold at the end of this
  story?

UP AND COMING/DOWN AND OUT

Mrs. Fielding: Good morning, Mrs. Gold.

Mrs. Gold: Good morning, Mrs. Fielding.

Mrs. Fielding: Now, isn't it about time you called me Anna?

Mrs. Gold: Yes. You're right. And my name is Rebecca, but call me Becky.

Mrs. Fielding: Becky, did you see the newspaper this morning?

Mrs. Gold: No, why?

Mrs. Fielding: There's an article about that boy on the roof. Wasn't that an awful thing?

Mrs. Gold: Terrible. What did it say?

Mrs. Fielding: I'll bring it down to you later, but he lived on 89th Street in the building in back of ours.

Mrs. Gold: He did? What was his name?

Mrs. Fielding: Henry diBernardo. Did you know him?

Mrs. Gold: No. It's funny. He lived right around the corner but I'd never seen him around here. The first time I saw him was when they brought him down. You know, down from the roof. He looked like Willie Dorio—the new tenant in 5W. Do you know him?

Mrs. Fielding: No. I haven't met him yet.

Mrs. Gold: You won't have long to wait. He's coming down the stairs now.

Mrs. Fielding: How do you know?

Mrs. Gold: Listen. He's coming down two steps at a time.

Mrs. Fielding: For goodness sake! You're right.

(Willie appears)

Mrs. Gold: *(to Mrs. F.)* You see?
(to Willie) Good morning, Willie.

Willie: Hi, Mrs. Gold.

Mrs. Gold: Willie, I'd like you to meet Mrs. Fielding in 3W. Mrs. Fielding, this is Willie Dorio.

Willie: Pleased to meet you.

Mrs. Fielding: *(turning to Mrs. G.)* Anyway, the funeral is this afternoon in that funeral home on Second Avenue. I think I remember him from the high school cafeteria. I work there, you know. He was a good kid—graduated just

	last June, I think.
Mrs. Gold:	It makes you wonder. Anna, why do kids *do* these things?
Willie:	Easy. There's no reason not to.
Mrs. Gold:	But you don't take drugs, Willie.
Willie:	The hard stuff? No. But you never know. Hey, listen. If I don't get to work, I'm going to get fired. *(to Mrs. F.)* Nice meeting you. *(looking back at Mrs. G.)* Don't look so worried. I can take care of myself.
Mrs. Fielding:	Bye, Willie.
Mrs. Gold:	Goodbye.

(Willie runs out.)

Mrs. Fielding:	So that's Willie. What does he do?
Mrs. Gold:	He's a salesman at Pretty Feet, you know, that shoe store on Third Avenue.
Mrs. Fielding:	Oh yes. I'll bet he's a real hit with the ladies. He must be making a good salary the way he dresses.
Mrs. Gold:	I guess so. By the way, how's your husband these days?
Mrs. Fielding:	George? He's fine. Same as ever.
Mrs. Gold:	And the girls?
Mrs. Fielding:	They're fine. Actually, we've been doing a lot of thinking about the girls lately.
Mrs. Gold:	Oh?
Mrs. Fielding:	Amanda will be going to high school next

fall, and George doesn't like what he hears.

Mrs. Gold:	About the schools?
Mrs. Fielding:	Yes.
Mrs. Gold:	Well, Anna, you work in the high school, what do you think?
Mrs. Fielding:	I don't know what to say. I believe in public education, but I don't want our girls going to McKinley High.
Mrs. Gold:	Things are that bad?
Mrs. Fielding:	Yes.
Mrs. Gold:	What are you going to do?
Mrs. Fielding:	You know how it is. You want to give your kids something better. We want to give our girls the advantages we didn't have. Well, I could talk all day. I'm on my way to the store. Can I get you anything?
Mrs. Gold:	To tell you the truth, I'm out of sugar and flour. They're too heavy for me to carry, you know.
Mrs. Fielding:	Oh. Let me get them for you.
Mrs. Gold:	Thank you, Anna. Here. Let me give you some money.
Mrs. Fielding:	No, that's all right. You can pay me later. Is that all?
Mrs Gold:	That's all, thanks. Just five pounds of sugar and five pounds of flour.
Mrs. Fielding:	Do you do a lot of baking?
Mrs. Gold:	No, but I think I'm going to do a lot more.

CULTURAL NOTES

It is complicated to explain how we decide whether to call a person by his first or last name.

In the story, both Mrs. Gold (who is older) and Willie Dorio (who is younger) call Anna Fielding by her last name. Older people often call younger people by their first names. But we usually have to be asked by older people to use their first names before we do it. Anna will probably call Mrs. Gold by her first name, Becky, from now on. If Mrs. Gold asked Willie to call her by her first name, he would probably have a more difficult time because he is so much younger.

In chapter seven, you will see that Willie Dorio meets Sally Gibson. They will call each other Willie and Sally right away because they are young, single, and about the same age.

In general, we like to be on a "first name basis" with one another. We feel it is friendlier. If someone asks you to call him by his first name, you should do it even if it is difficult for you. Otherwise, he'll think you're unfriendly.

The most difficult decisions we have to make with names are at work, at school, or with people with whom we deal professionally. Do you call your boss Jack or Mr. Brown? Do you call your teacher Maria or Ms. Melendez? If you are not sure, you can ask people what they prefer. Remember, only use Miss, Mrs., Ms., and Mr. with the person's last name.

In general, we like to use nicknames. It is a sign of affection and friendliness. Rebecca becomes Becky. William becomes Willie or Bill. Even President Carter preferred to use Jimmy as his first name instead of James.

When people have difficulty pronouncing your first name, they may want to change it to an American name. One of our friends whose name is Mohammed found that the Americans he worked with wanted to call him Mike. He decided to go along with that. Now most of his friends call him Mike. Another of our friends is named Panya. Some of his American friends at school began to call him Pat. He felt very strongly that he wanted to keep his Thai name and did not want to become Americanized. He just kept correcting his friends by asking them to call him Panya and finally they did. You should make your own decision. For those of you from Spanish-speaking countries, you should understand that there is one name that we have difficulty using. That name is *Jésus*. Americans feel uncomfortable calling anyone by that name. But they will not mind as much if they are helped to use the Spanish pronunciation.

- ***What are the customs for using names in your country?***

COMPREHENSION EXERCISES

Face the Facts

If the sentence is true, write "T." If the sentence is false, write "F."

1. ___ Henry diBernardo lived on 88th Street.

2. ___ Mrs. Gold had seen him before the police brought him down from the roof.

3. ___ Mrs. Fielding meets Willie Dorio in this story.

4. ___ Anna Fielding doesn't want her girls to go to McKinley High School.

5. ___ Mrs. Fielding agrees to buy some things for Mrs. Gold at the store.

Read Between the Lines

If the sentence is true, write "T." If the sentence is false, write "F." Make an inference.

1. ___ Henry diBernardo was about twenty-one years old when he died.

2. ___ The Fielding girls are giving their parents a lot of trouble.

3. ___ Mrs. Fielding feels strongly that McKinley High is a bad school.

4. ___ Mrs. Fielding believes it is good for people from all levels of society to mix together.

5. ___ Mrs. Gold is very weak physically.

Discussion Questions

Discuss the following questions with your classmates, or write your answers below.

1. When Mrs. Gold says, "But you don't take drugs, Willie," why doesn't Willie just answer, "No?"

2. If all schools were free, would you send your children to a private, public, or parochial school?

MORE DIFFICULT COMPREHENSION EXERCISES

Find the Supporting Details

1. Mrs. Fielding says that she read about the boy on

the roof in the paper. How do you know this is true?
List two things.

2. Mrs. Fielding says she thinks she remembers Henry
   diBernardo. What does she say that indicates this
   is true?

Make a Judgment

1. How do you think Mrs. Fielding feels about Willie?
   Discuss your answer and your reasons for it with
   your classmates.
2. How do you feel about Willie? Discuss your opinion
   and your reasons for it.

VOCABULARY EXERCISES
Mind Your Words

public
hit

for goodness sake
hard stuff

Look at the following exercises. They will help you
understand how these items are used. You may use your
dictionary to find their definitions. Remember, we are
working with the meaning of the items as they appear in
the dialogue. They may have other meanings in other
contexts.

PUBLIC
"I believe in *public* education, but I don't want my girls
going to McKinley High."

There are three definitions below. Which one means
the same as *public* as it is used in the sentence above?
   1. open to everyone
   2. private
   3. religious

In the United States, all the following institutions can
be public or private except one. Which one is it?
   1. schools
   2. hospitals
   3. churches
   4. museums

Which is *not* true? In the U.S., public high schools are:
   1. free (no tuition)
   2. open to everyone
   3. operated by the government
   4. more expensive than private schools

HIT

"I'll bet he's a real *hit* with the ladies."

Choose the appropriate synonyms for *hit* in this context.
1. animal
2. failure
3. popular man
4. success

All of the following can be good and successful. Only one cannot be a *hit*. Which is it?
1. a song
2. a book
3. a school
4. a movie

A *hit with the ladies* is probably *not*:
1. popular
2. good-looking
3. dumb
4. fun

FOR GOODNESS SAKE

"*For goodness sake.* You're right."

Choose one. When Anna uses the expression, *for goodness sake,* she is:
1. angry
2. surprised

3. upset
4. hurt

Note: *When we believe something is not true or something will not happen and then find out that it is true or did happen, we often use the expression* for goodness sake. *This expression is used more often by women than by men.*

HARD STUFF

"The *hard stuff?* No."

In this expression, *hard* means:
1. difficult
2. hard to get
3. strict
4. strong

Of the following, which expression uses the word *hard* in the same way as *hard stuff?*
1. hard luck
2. hard liquor
3. hard job

Write an example of hard liquor here: ___wisky___

Write an example of something alcoholic that is *not* hard liquor here: _____

THE FACTS OF LIFE

American Schools

In general, we can divide our system into public, parochial, and private education. Public education is either free or has a low tuition. Parochial schools are usually more expensive than public schools but cheaper than private schools. Parochial schools are run by a church, but you do not have to belong to the church to go to its school. Private schools are often the most expensive kind of education. They can cost several thousand dollars a year.

Look at this table:

Age of Student (If he/she studies continuously)	Type of Schooling	Grades	Final Degree Given
2-5 years old	Play Group Preschool Headstart Nursery School Day Care	—	—
5½ years old	Kindergarten	—	—
6-11 years old	Elementary School Grammar School Primary School	1-6	Elementary School Diploma (sometimes)
11-13 years old	Middle School	6-8	—
12-13 years old	Junior High School	7-8	

14-17 years old	High School Vocational High School Technical High School	9-12 High School Degree	High School Diploma Vocational Diploma Technical Diploma (Some states also give State Diplomas)
18-19 years old	Junior College Community College	13-14 2-Year College Degree	Associate Bachelor of Arts (A.B.A.) Associate Bachelor of Science (A.B.S.)
18-21 years old	College University	Bachelor's or College Degree	Bachelor of Arts (B.A.) Bachelor of Science (B.S. and other degrees)
From 1 to 3 years more studying	College University	Master's Degree	Master of Arts (M.A.) Master of Science (M.S. and some other degrees)
From 3 to 7 years more	College University	Doctorate	Doctor of Education (Ed.D.) Doctor of Philosophy (Ph.D. and some other degrees)

Mrs. Gold went to kindergarten and elementary school. She did not get a diploma.

Sally went to kindergarten, elementary school, junior high school, high school, and college. She graduated with a B.A. in English.

Emily, Sally's sister, graduated from college and then got an M.A. in elementary education.

OPTIONAL EXERCISES

You might like to do these exercises:

1. Compare the educational system in your country to the system in the U.S. What is the same? What is different?
2. Describe your education. Do you have any diplomas or degrees? Do you have any certificates from training programs or business schools? Write your education according to the U.S. system.

See supplementary exercises on page 150.

SIX SIX SIX SIX

Some questions you might like to discuss with your classmates:

Where did you meet most of your friends? At work? At church? At school?

Do you think that young men and young women should be formally introduced?

Do you think that chaperones are a good idea?

What are the dating customs in your country?

Say these words

after your teacher or after an American friend. You'll find these words in the story.

cake
chap'·er·one
class (social)
count on
dif'·fer·ent
fig'·ure
in·tro·duce'
look for
piece

rec'·i·pe
re·mind'
whis'·per

phrases
count on (*someone*)
find a way
get the door
Good luck.

Hi-ya.
in need
Leave it to (*person*).
sound good to (*person*)
take care of
work fast
Yoo hoo.

In this chapter, Willie asks Mrs. Gold to help him meet Sally Gibson.

As you read the story, think about these questions:

Why does Willie want to meet Sally?

Why does Willie ask Mrs. Gold to help him?

How long does it take for Mrs. Gold to arrange a meeting between Willie and Sally?

How does Willie feel just before he meets Sally?

A FRIEND IN NEED

(Later that evening, there's a knock on Mrs. Gold's door.)

Mrs. Gold: Who is it?

Willie: Me. Willie.

Mrs. Gold: What a nice surprise.
(She opens the door.)
Come on in. I was just about to make a cup of coffee. And I baked a cake this afternoon. It's a new recipe. You'll have to tell me if you like it. You can't tell from reading the recipe, you know, if it's going to be any good or not. It's

chocolate. Do you like chocolate?

Willie: Sounds good to me.

Mrs. Gold: Come on in the kitchen.

(They go into the kitchen.)

Have a seat.

(Willie sits down, and Mrs. Gold gives him a piece of cake.)

Willie: Mrs. Gold, you know everyone in the building, don't you?

Mrs. Gold: I think so.

Willie: Who is the blond, about twenty-one, on the third floor? She lives with that older lady. You know the one.

Mrs. Gold: Yes. That's Sally and Emily.

Willie: Which one's which?

Mrs. Gold: What?

Willie: Which is the younger one?

Mrs. Gold: Sally. Sally's the blond you asked about first.

Willie: Sally. Yeah. She's got class.

Mrs. Gold: She's a very nice girl. She just graduated from college, you know, and she's looking for a job.

Willie: Good luck. Uh . . . I . . . uh . . . Would you . . . ?

Mrs. Gold: Would I what?

Willie: You know. This Sally. Could you . . . uh . . . ?

Mrs. Gold: Would you like me to introduce you?

Willie: Yeah. How did you know? I never asked anybody to introduce me before. But I figure this one's different.

Mrs. Gold: She's a little older than you are, you know.

Willie: I know it, and you know it, but she doesn't

Mrs. Gold: You remind me so much of a young man who used to live in the building.

Willie: Was he as good looking?

Mrs. Gold: He'd say so. Anyway, leave it to me. I'll find a way to introduce you two.

Willie: Great. I knew I could count on you. Thanks.

(Willie leaves and then comes back just before the door closes.)

Hey, Mrs. Gold! Great cake!

Mrs. Gold: Glad you liked it!

(The next morning, Mrs. Gold sees Willie leaving the building. She opens her window and calls to him.)

Mrs. Gold: Yoo hoo! Willie!

Willie: Hi-ya, Mrs. Gold. Can't talk. Got to run. I'm late for work already.

Mrs. Gold: Sally's going to be here tonight at 8:30. You can meet her then.

Willie: Wow! You work fast. Thanks a lot. See you at 8:30.

(That night at 8:30, there's a knock on Mrs. Gold's door. She opens it.)

Willie: *(whispering)* Is she here? How do I look?

Mrs. Gold: Beautiful.

Willie: Come on. Where is she?

Mrs. Gold:	They're not here yet.
Willie:	*They?*
Mrs. Gold:	Yes. Emily is coming, too.
Willie:	You've got to be kidding. I don't need another chaperone. One's enough.
Mrs. Gold:	Willie!

Willie:	You know what I mean.
Mrs. Gold:	Don't worry. I'll take care of Emily.
Willie:	Where is she? Hey! Are you sure she's coming?
Mrs. Gold:	They'll be here. Why don't you sit down?

(There's a knock on the door. Willie jumps up.)

CULTURAL NOTES

1. When we describe people, we usually go from top to bottom. We begin with the hair and the face (he has dark hair, a round face, big eyes, he's fat).
   - *How do you describe people in your country?*

2. When we meet a person for the first time, it is not unusual to ask the following questions: Where do you live? What do you do for a living? Are you married? Do you have any children? and, sometimes, Where did you go to school? In this story, Mrs. Gold describes Sally by stating that she is a college graduate and is looking for a job.
   - *What do you usually want to know first? Is it okay to ask these questions in your country?*

3. In many countries, when you meet someone you know, you must stand and speak to them for a minute or two, no matter how busy you are. In the U.S., we often wave, shout "hello," and keep on going. We feel that it is very important to be on time for work or for appointments. Willie shouts to Mrs. Gold, "Can't talk. I'm late for work." She understands and is not bothered by this.
   - *How would you feel if someone did this to you? Would you like it?*

COMPREHENSION EXERCISES

Face the Facts

If the sentence is true, write "T." If the sentence is false, write "F."

1. ___ Willie wants to meet Sally.

2. ___ Willie wants Mrs. Gold to introduce him to Emily.

3. ___ Sally and Emily are late.

4. ___ Mrs. Gold is sure that Sally and Emily are coming.

5. ___ Willie likes Mrs. Gold's cake.

MORE DIFFICULT COMPREHENSION EXERCISES

Read Between the Lines

If the sentence is true, write "T." If the sentence is false, write "F." Make an inference.

1. ___ Willie usually has someone introduce him to girls he wants to meet.

2. ___ Sally is different from most of the girls Willie knows.

3. ___ Willie didn't expect that Mrs. Gold would be able to arrange a meeting so quickly.

4. ___ Willie is nervous about meeting Sally.

5. ___ Willie is happy that Emily is coming with Sally.

Find the Supporting Details

Mrs. Gold says that she knows everyone in the building. Give some examples from this story or other stories to show this is true.

Make a Judgment

Willie says to Mrs. Gold, "I knew I could count on you." Do you think that Willie can really count on Mrs. Gold? Why or why not?

VOCABULARY EXERCISES

Mind Your Words

class

good luck

Look at the following exercises. They will help you understand how these items are used. You may use your dictionary to find their definitions. Remember, we are working with the meaning of the items as they appear in the dialogue. They may have other meanings in other contexts.

CLASS
"She's got *class.*"

In the sentence above, *class* has a:
1. positive meaning
2. negative meaning
3. neutral meaning

In the sentence above, *class* refers to:
1. classrooms
2. a diploma
3. social class

Which of the following may give a person *class*?
1. a lot of money
2. a good education
3. an important family
4. good manners
5. good food
6. health
7. an expensive house

Discuss your answers with your classmates.

GOOD LUCK
Mrs. Gold: . . . she's looking for a job.
Willie: *Good luck.*

Usually we wish *good luck* directly to the person who needs it. We say both words equally: Good′ luck′. In the sentence above, Willie says *good luck* but he is being funny. He says it like this: G-o-o-o-d luck′. Ask your teacher or an American friend to say it for you.

Among the sentences below, find the one that says what Willie means when he says, "Good luck."
1. I hope she gets a job.
2. I think she'll find a job soon.
3. I hope she'll be lucky.
4. I think she'll have a hard time finding a job.

THE FACTS OF LIFE

A Recipe

In this chapter, Mrs. Gold makes a chocolate cake for Willie. Just for fun, here's a recipe for chocolate cake.

Maybe you could make it and bring it to class; or perhaps, you could all make it as a class.

Notice the following abbreviations:

lb.	= pound
oz.	= ounce
tsp.	= teaspoon
tbsp.	= tablespoon
in.	= inch
pkg.	= package
° F	= degrees Farenheit

Ingredients for cake:
  2 cups boiling water
  1 cup unsweetened cocoa
  2¾ cups sifted all-purpose flour
  2 tsp. baking soda
  ½ tsp. salt
  ½ tsp. baking powder
  1 cup butter or margarine, softened
  2½ cups granulated sugar
  4 eggs
  1½ tsp. vanilla extract

Ingredients for frosting:
  1 pkg. (6 oz.) semisweet chocolate
  ½ cup light cream
  1 cup butter or margarine
  2½ cups unsifted confectioners' sugar

Ingredients for filling:

  1 cup heavy cream, chilled
  ¼ cup unsifted confectioners' sugar
  1 tsp. vanilla extract

In a bowl, combine cocoa and boiling water, mixing until smooth. Cool completely.

Sift flour with soda, salt, and baking powder.

Preheat oven to 350° F.

Grease well and lightly flour *three* 9 in. by 1½ in. layer cake pans.

In a large bowl, use an electric mixer at high speed to beat butter, sugar, eggs, and vanilla for about five minutes until light.

Divide the flour mixture into four parts. Divide the cocoa mixture into three parts. At a low speed, beat in one part of the flour mixture, then one part of the cocoa mixture, until all is combined. Do not beat too long.

Divide this evenly into three pans. Make the tops smooth. Bake twenty-five to thirty minutes, or until the top of the cake springs back when you press with your finger.

Cool in the pans for about ten minutes. Take the cake out of the pans carefully and cool them on a rack.

Frosting: In a pan, combine chocolate pieces, cream, and butter. Stir over medium heat until smooth. Remove from heat. Blend in the confectioners' sugar. Put the bowl in ice and beat the mixture until it holds its shape.

Filling: Beat the cream with sugar and vanilla. Refrigerate.

To put the cake together: Place a layer on a plate, top side down. Spread with half the cream. Place a second layer, top side down, on the first. Spread with the rest of the cream. Place the third layer, top side up.

To frost: Cover the sides completely with frosting. Use the rest of the frosting on the top. Refrigerate one hour before serving.

Do you have a favorite recipe? Share it with your classmates.

See supplementary exercises on page 151.

SEVENSEVENSEVEN

Some questions you might like to discuss with your classmates:

What do you like to do in the evenings? Visit friends? Go to a movie? Go dancing?

What things don't you like to do?

When you go out, do you like to do new things?

Say these words

after your teacher or after an American friend.

bet	neck	cheer up
dan'·cing	po·lite'	know the score
dis'·co	some' place	pain in the neck
es·pres'·so	type (kind)	suit (*reflexive*)
kind (of)		You can say that a·gain'.
La'·tin	*phrases*	
mid'·dle	call off	

In this chapter, Willie and Sally learn more about each other and try to find something they both would like to do that evening.

As you read the story, think about these questions:

Why does Willie want to get out of Mrs. Gold's apartment with Sally?
Where does Willie want to take Sally?
What does Sally want to do?
Why does Willie get angry with Sally?
Where do they finally go?

SCORING

(A few hours later, Willie and Sally are leaving the building together.)

Willie: Boy, am I glad to get out of there! I can't be polite for more than ten minutes at a time.
Sally: Really?
Willie: Yeah. It gives me a headache.
Sally: You should try it more often. You know, Mrs. Gold likes you, and I think Emily does, too.
Willie: Mrs. Gold's okay. She knows the score.
Sally: How do you like Emily?

Willie: She's . . . .

Sally: Go ahead. Say it!

Willie: She's not my type.

Sally: She thinks she has to take care of me. You know how older sisters are.

Willie: They're a pain in the . . . neck.
Hey, where do you want to go? There's a Latin disco on 86th Street.

Sally: Oh. I . . . .

Willie: What's the matter? Don't you like disco?

Sally: I'm not really very good at . . . .

Willie: Where do you come from?

Sally: Athol, Massachusetts.

Willie: Where's that?

Sally: In the middle of Massachusetts.

Willie: Never heard of it.

Sally: Most people haven't. But I can tell you we don't do much Latin disco dancing there.

Willie: I'll teach you. You're not too old to learn.

Sally: Nice of you to notice. Maybe some other time. How about going someplace where we can talk?

Willie: Talk? How about my apartment?

Sally: I said "talk."

Willie: Hey! What kind of a guy do you think I am? You don't know anything about me. Just because I didn't go to college doesn't mean that I'm an animal.

Sally: Maybe we'd better call the whole thing off.

Willie: Suit yourself.

Sally: Look. I don't want to go to your apartment, okay? Why don't we walk over to 86th Street for some espresso?

Willie: Sure.

Sally: Cheer up. You might even make a friend.

Willie: I have plenty of friends.

Sally: I'll bet they're not like me.

Willie: You can say that again.

CULTURAL NOTES

1. Sally makes several sarcastic comments to Willie. They begin with:

   You should . . .

   Nice . . .

   You might . . .

   Sally's use of sarcasm doesn't mean that she doesn't like Willie. It is clear that they like each other. But Sally is using sarcasm to put Willie in his place, to show him he's not the boss. Men and women in the U.S. often "fence" this way when they first meet. "Fencing" establishes the rules of the relationship. Willie may have expected Sally to be more traditional—to respond shyly to his complimentary remarks—and respect his wishes.
   - *How do you feel about Willie's attitude?*

2. At one time in the U.S., a young woman would never allow a young man to come into her apartment or house without a chaperone or friend around. Today, in urban areas, she might invite him in if she likes the man and trusts him.

3. In many countries a young woman would never be alone in a house with a young man. The standards of what makes a person "good" change from culture to culture. You may find people in America doing things you think are wrong. You might want to find out if other Americans think they are wrong, too, before you decide if the people are behaving correctly or not.
   - *What are the customs in your country?*

COMPREHENSION EXERCISES

Face the Facts

If the sentence is true, write "T." If the sentence is false, write "F."

1. ___ Willie is happy to get out of Mrs. Gold's apartment.

2. ___ Sally doesn't want Willie to teach her to disco dance right now.

3. ___ Sally wants to talk to Willie in his apartment.

4. ___ Willie has no friends.

5. ___ Most of Willie's friends are just like Sally.

Read Between the Lines

If the sentence is true, write "T." If the sentence is false, write "F." Make an inference.

1. ___ Willie likes Emily a lot.

2. ___ Sally doesn't know how to disco.

3. ___ Sally thinks Willie will want to talk if they go to his apartment.

4. ___ At the end of the story, they are going to go to a coffeehouse.

5. ___ Willie doesn't want to be Sally's friend.

MORE DIFFICULT COMPREHENSION EXERCISES
Find the Supporting Details

Sally annoys Willie. Read the story again, and notice what she does or says to upset his plans. List them here:

_____

_____

_____

_____

Make a Judgment

Sally and Willie have not made a smooth start. Do you think they will become friends? Do you think they will fall in love? Discuss your opinion and your reasons for it with other students.

VOCABULARY EXERCISES
Mind Your Words

know the score
kind of

type

Look at the following exercises. They will help you understand how these items are used. You may use your dictionary to find their definitions. Remember, we are working with the meanings of the items as they appear in the dialogue. They may have other meanings in other contexts.

KNOW THE SCORE
"Mrs. Gold's okay. She *knows the score.*"

In this context, *She knows the score* has a:
1. positive meaning
2. negative meaning
3. neutral meaning

She knows the score means:

1. She knows the number of points each team has.
2. She knows the person who is going to win.
3. She knows a lot about life.

When Willie says this, he is:

1. giving Mrs. Gold a compliment
2. complaining about Mrs. Gold
3. making fun of Mrs. Gold

If a person is always getting fired, do you think that this person *knows the score*?

1. Yes
2. No

We know a person. People are always going to her for information and advice. Do you think that this person probably *knows the score*?

1. Yes
2. No

Think of someone you know who *knows the score*. What does he or she know? What kinds of things would you go to him/her for? Write your answers here or discuss them with your classmates.

_____

_____

_____

KIND OF

"What *kind of* guy do you think I am?"

In the sentences below, only two of the underlined phrases are synonyms for *kind of*. Which ones are they?

1. What *type of* guy do you think I am?
2. What *sort of* guy do you think I am?
3. What *class of* guy do you think I am?
4. What *group of* guy do you think I am?

When Willie says, "What *kind of* guy do you think I am?" he is:

1. angry with Sally
2. happy with Sally
3. asking Sally a question

When Willie asks this question,

1. he expects Sally to answer it
2. he is telling her that she doesn't know him

When Willie asks this question,

1. he hopes Sally will explain what she knows about him
2. he hopes Sally will apologize for what she said or was thinking before

If someone asked Sally, "What kind of guy is Willie?" she would probably *first*:

1. describe his occupation

2. tell people where he lives
3. describe his personality and character
4. describe what Willie looks like

TYPE

"She's not my *type*."

Look at *my type* in the sentence above. Choose the sentence below which best states what Willie probably meant.
   1. She's not from the same social class as I am.
   2. She's not the kind of person whose appearance I like.
   3. She's not the kind of person whose personality I like.
   4. She's not from the same age group I am.

If a person is not your *type*, does it mean that she or he is not a nice person?
   1. Yes
   2. No

You just saw a car, and you said, "That's my type of car!" Describe the car.

You just saw a movie, and you said, "That's not my type of movie." Describe the movie.

You met someone for the first time, talked about ten minutes, and you said, "She (He) is not my type." Describe the person.

A slang expression used in informal situations to describe things you like or don't like is "That's (not) my bag." Example:

Willie: What are you into these days?
Nate: Jogging. I run about three miles a day. What about you?
Willie: Yeah, well, good for you. Running's not my *bag*. Now dancing . . . that's more my thing.

This expression is often used by young people these days.

THE FACTS OF LIFE

A Job Interview

Sometimes a job interviewer will "fence" with you. He or she will ask you a difficult question or make a comment to see how you respond to it. Each person has to answer these questions in his/her own way. Sometimes it helps to have thought about some possible answers in advance. You will want to have a clever answer, but one that is not too impolite or aggressive.

EXERCISES

Here are some examples of difficult questions that an American job interviewer might ask a non-native speaker of English. Write or discuss possible responses. Before you respond, think of what the interviewer is looking for in your answer.

1. Why did you come to this country? Didn't you like your own country?
2. How would you feel about working for a woman?
3. I've been listening to you speak. Do you know that you make mistakes when you speak English?
4. You don't have very much work experience in this country, do you?
5. Why should I hire you for this job?
6. I'm not sure you are qualified for this job.
7. What's more important to you—your family or your career?
8. I hear that they don't like Americans in your country. Is this true?

See supplementary exercises on pages 152 and 163.

Some questions you might like to discuss with your classmates:

Are you satisfied with your present occupation, or would you like to do something else?

What kind of job would you like to have?

How do most people find jobs?

Say these words

after your teacher or after an American friend.

a'·gen·cy	ed'·i·tor	smart
as·sis'·tant	* em·ploy'·ment	*split
bud'·dy	ex·cuse' (n.)	test
†ca·reer'	field	wait'·er
catch (n.)	point	*what·ev'·er
check (n.) (bill)	quite	
coun'·sel·or	*re·fer'	

*split (insert)

phrases

B.A.	look for a nee'·dle in a hay'·stack
check _something_ out	out there
for sure	put + (_someone_) + down _insult_
Have it your way.	What's the catch?

In this chapter, Sally and Willie talk about finding the right job.

As you read the story, think about these questions:

What kind of a job is Sally looking for?
Why hasn't she found one?
Why hasn't Willie found a better job?
What does Sally suggest he do?
Why does Sally want to split the bill?

A NEEDLE IN A HAYSTACK

(Later, at the coffeehouse on 86th Street.)

Willie: So, now you know the whole story.
Sally: That's quite a story. I can see why you felt you had to leave home. What now?
Willie: I don't know. I'm not going to sell shoes all my life, that's for sure. But I don't know what I want to do.

Sally: Hey. At least you've got a job. I've been looking for something for a month. Wherever I go they say, "What can you do?" And all I can say is that I've got a B.A. in English. I want to be an editor, but you can't walk in and *be* an editor. You have to be an assistant editor first. But that's not the point. There are thousands of people like me with B.A.s in English and only a few jobs.

Willie: At least you know what you want to be. And you're smart. You can always learn what you don't know. But what about me? Maybe there's a job out there. You know, one that I would really like. But how am I supposed to know?

Sally: Don't put yourself down so much. Why don't you go to an employment counselor? They give you tests to find out what you like and what you can do. Have you ever thought of that?

Willie: An employment agency?

Sally: No, a counselor. Agencies will just refer you to whatever jobs they have. They don't usually tell you what field to look in.

Willie: What's the catch? Are these counselors expensive?

Sally: I don't know. Why don't you check it out? It can't hurt.

Willie: I guess not.

(to the waiter)

The check, please.

(to Sally)

But what if I have to go to school?

Sally: So? You can go at night. Stop making excuses. You can do anything you want to do.

Willie: Yeah. I can be the first President from the Bronx.

Sally: You can also make a career of feeling sorry for yourself.

(The waiter brings the check, and Sally takes it.)

Willie: Hey! What are you doing?

Sally: What do you do with the bill when you go out with your buddies?

Willie: Split it.

Sally: Okay. That's what I'm doing.

Willie: Have it your way. Women!

Sally: What about them?

Willie: You can't figure them.

Sally: Come on. You love us the way we are.

Willie: If you only knew. Let's go.

COMPREHENSION EXERCISES
Face the Facts

If the sentence is true, write "T." If the sentence is false, write "F."

1. ___ Willie doesn't want to sell shoes for the rest of his life.

2. ___ It's easy to find a job as an editor.

3. ___ An employment counselor and an employment agency are the same thing.

4. ___ Sally thinks Willie is making too many excuses for himself.

5. ___ Willie agrees to split the check with Sally.

Read Between the Lines

If the sentence is true, write "T." If the sentence is false, write "F." Make an inference.

1. ___ Willie knew about employment counselors before Sally told him about them.

2. ___ Willie thinks Sally is smarter than he is.

3. ___ Sally knows all about employment counselors.

4. ___ Willie believes he can do anything he wants to do.

5. ___ Willie wants to go Dutch with Sally.

MORE DIFFICULT COMPREHENSION EXERCISES

Find the Supporting Details

Employment agencies and employment counselors are not the same thing. Find the information in the story that shows that this statement is true. What does each one do?

Make a Judgment

Sally is not the kind of woman that Willie usually goes out with. Do you think it is possible for them to be friends?

VOCABULARY EXERCISES

Mind Your Words

   quite
    field
   make a career of

Look at the following exercises. They will help you understand how these items are used. You may use your dictionary to find their definitions. Remember, we are working with the meanings of the items as they appear in the dialogue. They may have other meanings in other contexts.

QUITE

"That's *quite* a story."

Another way to say *quite a story* is:
   1. an unusual story
   2. a very long story
   3. a little story
   4. an extraordinary story

Quite, in this context, is:
   1. a positive word
   2. a negative word
   3. a neutral word

Very often, we don't say what we really feel because we don't want to hurt people or because it is not appropriate to condemn other people's customs or actions. For example:

A person tells you that in his country people drink snakes' blood. (This is, in fact, a custom in parts of Southeast Asia.) What do you say?

1. The whole idea of drinking snakes' blood makes me sick.
2. I'd love to have some.
3. That's an interesting custom.
4. Let's change the subject.

Think back to the dialogue. How does Sally respond to Willie's story? What kind of story do you think it is?

FIELD

"They won't tell you what *field* to look in."

As used in the sentence above, a good synonym for *field* is:
1. area of specialization or employment
2. place where you play baseball
3. farm land
4. factory or office

What fields are you interested in?

What fields have you already had experience in?

Look at the following list. On the left is the occupation, on the right, write the field. You can work in a group with several classmates if you wish.

doctor	*medicine*
teacher	*education*
plumber	service

piano player	Music
businessman	business
practical nurse	nursing
banker	banking

MAKE A CAREER OF

"You can *make a career of* feeling sorry for yourself."

In the sentence above, Sally is being:
1. sarcastic
2. optimistic
3. realistic

When Sally suggests that Willie is making a career of feeling sorry for himself, she is saying that he:
1. learned to feel sorry for himself in school
2. has a lot a skill in feeling sorry for himself
3. has been feeling sorry for himself for too long a time
4. has a job that helps him feel sorry for himself

Look just at the word *career*. All the following are *careers* except one. Which one is it?
1. teaching
2. feeling sorry for yourself
3. law
4. medicine
5. accounting

THE FACTS OF LIFE
Employment Agencies and Counselors

When people go to an *employment agency,* they will tell the interviewer what skills they have, what kind of job they are looking for, what kind of salary they would like, and, frequently, the size and location of the company or institution they want to work for. The purpose of the agency is to match the right person with the right job. Fees vary from under $100.00 to several hundred dollars. The fee for the agency's service depends on several things. Sometimes the person who is looking for the job pays the fee. There can be a flat fee—the person has to pay this fee to the agency before he gets any help. There can also be a split fee—the person has to pay some money in advance and the rest in monthly installments after he gets a job. Or the agency can charge 10-15 percent of your first year's salary after they get you a job.

Problem: If you get a job through an agency and your first year's salary is $10,000, how much will you have to pay the agency if their fee is 15% of your first year's salary? How much would that be each month? Would you use this agency again, or do you think they charge too much?

Sometimes the fee is paid by the company that is doing the hiring. In this case, you would not have to pay anything for the agency's service. If you cannot afford to pay a fee, only look for "fee paid" positions.
Employment counselors are different from employment agencies. A person who goes to a job counselor is usually unhappy with what he is doing, but does not really know what else to do. Sometimes people who have had a general education (they have not studied for a particular occupation) go to counselors to help them find a field they could be interested in.

An employment counselor tries to find out what you would like and what your talents are. He then tries to find a field you would be successful in.

To do this, some counselors give a number of psychological tests to find out what you can do well and what you like to do. Other counselors ask you to recall the happiest or most satisfying moments of your life and then they help you find an occupation that will include similar satisfying moments. After this, the counselor may refer you to people in the new field. You will have appointments with these people to talk to them about their jobs. Then you can decide if you want to try to find employment in this new field. Very often the contacts you have made through the people you meet in these appointments will lead to a job offer.

Look at the following ads:

HELP WANTED

ACCOUNTANCY $20M

MAJOR CONGLOMERATE
Deg acctant. Wall St exp. Having handled performance reports of funds. Excel growth. Nr. Penn Central.   CALL

H. PETER   555-3200

Bway Suite 1117 Agency

This is an ad that was placed by an agency. They do not mention the fee. You will probably have to pay the fee yourself. You can't tell the name of this Wall Street company from the ad. You are only told that this is a large company. Some people prefer to work for a big company because it probably will not go out of business.

Abbreviations:

M = thousand
Deg acctant = a degree in accounting
exp = experience
Excel = excellent
Nr. = near

Abbreviations:

CPA = certified public accountant

Sr. = senior (this means well-trained with several years experience and good skills)

Reqs. = requires

This ad is called a "blind ad." You will have to send a resume to the newspaper at the box number indicated. You'll need to call the newspaper (here it's the *Tribune*) and ask for the newspaper's address. You should write a letter and enclose a copy of this ad with your resume.

This ad was placed by an agency, and indicates that the fee will be paid by the company.

Abbreviations:

Pd = paid   acctg = accounting

Oppty = opportunity

Abbreviations:

bkgrd = background

pref'd = preferred

misc = miscellaneous

Ext. = extension

This ad was probably placed by the company. If you are interested in this job, you will have to call the phone number given in the ad to find out what they want you to do next.

```
┌─────────────────────────────┐
│        TRAVEL AGENT         │
│  Must be experienced. Queens│
│  location open. Salary & bene-│
│  fits.   Call Jeanne Klein  │
│    METROPOLITAN TRAVEL      │
│         555-1100            │
└─────────────────────────────┘
```

In this ad you know the name of the company, Metropolitan Travel; its location, Queens; the person you will need to talk to, Jeanne Klein; and the number to call.

Look at the following ads and answer the following questions about as many of them as you wish:

> Is this an agency ad?
> Is the fee paid or not?
> What kind of job is it?
> What qualifications are required, if any?
> Is the salary mentioned?
> What do you have to do to answer the ad?

1.

```
┌─────────────────────────────┐
│        ACCOUNTING           │
│          CLERKS             │
│                             │
│  Immediate openings for indi-│
│  viduals with minimum 6 college│
│  accounting credits. Previous│
│  figure clerk experience and │
│  good phone ability.        │
│                             │
│  Position provides excellent │
│  starting salary and full com-│
│  pany paid benefits in modern│
│  offices convenient to all trans-│
│  portation.                 │
│                             │
│   Apply in Person 9-11A.M.  │
│       or 2-4P.M.            │
│                             │
│      24th FLOOR             │
│   1520 Washington Street    │
│  Equal Opportunity Employer │
│           M/F               │
└─────────────────────────────┘
```

Abbreviations:
  M/F = male or female

2.

```
┌─────────────────────────────┐
│      TRAVEL AGENT EXPD      │
│  Min 3-4 yrs. exp. domestic &│
│  intl Sal commens w/exp.    │
│  555-6140        Mr. Overton│
└─────────────────────────────┘
```

Abbreviations:
  Expd = experienced
  Min = minimum
  intl = international
  Sal commens w/exp. =
    Salary commensurate
    with experience (more
    experience = higher salary)

3.

```
┌─────────────────────────────┐
│   TRAVEL REPRESENTATIVES    │
│  The time is right! Travel oppor-│
│  tunities galore! High commis-│
│  sions, free travel benefits. For│
│  ambitious exp'd & non-exp'd │
│  people free training for be-│
│  ginners.      Call Mr. Taylor│
│           555-7065          │
└─────────────────────────────┘
```

4.

```
┌─────────────────────────────┐
│     ACCOUNTING CLERK        │
│                             │
│  A leading international firm of│
│  consulting engineers in mid-│
│  town area has opening in ac-│
│  counting section for individ-│
│  ual interested in analyzing diversi-│
│  fied contracts and preparing│
│  invoices accordingly. Compa-│
│  rable experience preferred. Sub-│
│  mit resume of qualifications│
│  and salary requirements to: │
│                             │
│     BOX 40 INQUIRER         │
│                             │
│   An Equal Opportunity      │
│     Employer M/F            │
└─────────────────────────────┘
```

5.

ACCOUNTING CLERK
FEE PAID
$150 to $200

Major Midtown Company offers Jr. position in all Phases Accounts Receivable. Req. six months + experience in Department Store &/or a Manufacturer's Accounting Dept: Doing either A/R or A/P or Claims Adjusting is necessary. Experience in any one of these OK. Company offers an excellent benefits package including tuition refund.

A & M

AGENCY ASSOCIATES
902 BROADWAY 17th FL.
555-4500

Abbreviations:
Jr. = Junior (less experienced)
Dept = department
A/R = Accounts Receivable
A/P = Accounts Payable
Fl. = floor

6.

TRAVEL $11-12,000
STAFF ASS'T

Act as liaison between Co & Hotel caterers & Airlines. Set up conventions. Good skills required. All benefits including free travel to San Francisco.
FEE PAID
Call: BILL HACKETT
555-5000
JORAM Agency
150 West Street

Abbreviations:
Ass't = assistant
Co = company

7.

SOUND ENGINEER FOR TOURING ROCK BAND

At least 1 year experience. Reply D. Sampson, 915 Lincoln Blvd. Boston, MA

Abbreviations:
MA = Massachusetts

8.

TREEMAN (m/f) Climbers & Groundmen

$50,000

Do you make $50,000/yr min or are you starving in winter & busting your back in summer? We have work yr-round, 365 days/year, & make money. If you have the equipment, know how to work, and are willing to relocate with equipment, call:

JORGINS CORP.
Slim Jim's Tree Svc
813-555-3700

No Collect Calls Accepted

Abbreviations:
/yr = per year
min = minimum
svc = service

9.

Ger/Eng Secy/Admin Ass't for intl trading firm. Good skills & knowl of all phases of purchasing. F/pd $325
LINGUA ltd.
BILINGUAL SPECIALISTS
Rm 1805 12 East 60th St.
(agency)   555-4901

Abbreviations:
Ger = German
Eng = English
secy = secretary
Admin = administrative
knowl = knowledge
F/pd = fee paid
ltd. = limited
Rm = room

10.

Airline Mechanic
With minimum 2 yrs experience on DC8 & DC10 aircraft. Contact D. Vernam, International Airways, Inc., JFK International Airport.
212-555-7400

11.

```
TRAVEL AGENTS F/P $11M+
BKLYN., QNS., L.I.
Minimum 2 yrs Vacation or
Comml exp.
Best opportunities in these
areas.
TRAVEL MASTERS, INC.
300 DIX DRIVE 555-7720
9th Flr        8 A.M.-6 P.M.
agency
```

Abbreviations:
  Bklyn. = Brooklyn
  Qns. = Queens
  L.I. = Long Island
  Comml = commercial
  Flr = floor

12.

```
Key Punch, disk, CRT's Spots
Mid/downtown Temp./Perm.
Good benefits.
NO FEE        To about $225
Rm 1401, 1B Agency 505 5 Av.
555-0345
```

Abbreviations:
  Temp. = temporary
  Perm. = permanent

13.

```
GAL/GUY FRI
Midtown to $10M
SOCIAL WORK RESEARCH
Orgzd person w min one yr ofc
exp Typ 60 + own corresp;
young staff

PINEZICH Agency 90 W 52 St.
555-5030
```

Abbreviations:
  Gal/Guy Fri = Gal or
    Guy Friday (a woman
    or a man who does
    all kinds of work)
  Orgzd = organized
  w = with
  ofc = office
  Typ 60+ = can type 60
    words a minute or more
  own corresp = can write
    good letters by him or
    herself

14.

```
CHEF
Immediate opening fr expd
Italian Chef, new yr-round
restrnt. Rm & Brd, good
salary, health ins., paid vac-
ation incl. Call or write owner/
mgr.
Box 62 Wilmington VT. 05363;
          802-555-6394
```

Abbreviations:
  fr = for
  restrnt = restaurant
  Rm & Brd = room and
    board (a place to
    sleep and all meals)
  ins. = insurance
  incl = included
  mgr = manager

15.

```
GAL/GUY FRI. Excel oppty in
media dep't of large midtown
adv agency. Typing 50wpm,
some statistical typing.
Call 555-6530
```

Abbreviations:
  dep't = department
  adv = advertising
  wpm = words per
    minute

Look back at all the ads. Even if you like your job, is there any job there that you would like to have? If yes, tell your classmates which one it is, and why you would like it.

See supplementary exercises on page 153.

NINENINENINENINE

Some questions you might like to discuss with your classmates:

Do (or did) you live in a house or an apartment in your country?

Which do you think is better—a house or an apartment? Why?

Are houses expensive in your country? About how much would a nice house cost (in dollars)?

Say these words

after your teacher or after an American friend.

a·go'	men'·tion	*phrases*
ap·ply'	mis·take'	be in·vol'·ved with
base'·ball	prac'·tice	down pay'·ment
blame	price	get by
both'·er	pro·mo'·tion	get in'·to
chin	re·tire'·ment	grow up
co'·lor	score (test)	Keep *(something)* from
de·pend'	steak	*(someone)*.
dim'·ple	stew	let go
doll	su'·per·mar·ket	Post Of'·fice
dream'·y	trans'·fer	set an ex·am'·ple
gor'·geous	up·set'	What for?
harm'·less	va'·ry	
in·fla'·tion		*slang*
in'·terest (v.)		bug *(someone)*
lone'·ly		yup

In this chapter, George and Anna Fielding discuss their children and their future. They would like to escape their problems.

As you read the story, think about these questions:

What is Amanda interested in these days?
Why is her mother worried about her?
Why does Anna Fielding want to move?
Why are the Fieldings having stew for dinner?
Who did Anna Fielding invite over after dinner?

MAKING A BREAK

(Amanda is coming home from school. She opens the door of Apartment 3W.)

Amanda: Hi, Mom.
Anna: You're late today, Amanda. Where have you been? It's almost five o'clock.
Amanda: We were watching the boys at baseball practice.
Anna: Who's "we?"
Amanda: Some of us girls.
Anna: Who?
Amanda: You don't know them.
Anna: How is that nice Cynthia Miles from church?
Amanda: Boring.
Anna: Amanda!

Amanda: Well, she is. Oh, Mom, did you see that gorgeous new man in 5W? What a doll!
Anna: Amanda! Enough of that talk.
Amanda: Oh, but Mom. He's so cool. And did you see the dimple on his chin? He's dreamy.
Anna: And white.
Amanda: I know that.
Anna: Do you? Why don't you dream about some nice black boy?
Amanda: Why are you picking on me today?
Anna: He's involved with the boy who got murdered on the roof, you know. He's not for you. And he's not our kind.
Amanda: Don't you always say it doesn't matter what color you are if you're a nice person?
Anna: Yes, honey. I do. I guess . . . I guess I just don't want you to get hurt.
Amanda: I won't get hurt.
(Anna smiles.)
Anna: Tell me about those dreamy boys at baseball practice.

(An hour later, the door slams.)

Anna: George, is that you?
George: Yup.

(George comes in and kisses Anna.)

Anna: Well, did you hear anything?

George: Not a word.

Anna: Oh, well. You got the highest score, and the bosses like you.

George: I know, Anna, but the Post Office doesn't work that way. They don't have to take the person with the highest test score.

Anna: If you don't get the promotion, why don't you apply for a transfer?

George: What's gotten into you today?

Anna: Why not apply?

George: Where? What for? What about *your* job?

Anna: Oh, I can always get another.

George: You can, can you? What's really bothering you?

Anna: I don't know. I think I'm upset about Amanda. She's growing up so quickly.

George: What did she do?

Anna: She didn't do anything, really. The only thing that interests her is boys.

George: That's not so strange.

Anna: But she's only thirteen. She was out 'til five o'clock watching the boys play baseball.

George: That sounds pretty harmless to me.

Anna: And then she couldn't stop talking about that boy on the top floor.

George: He's a good-looking kid.

Anna: You're as bad as she is.

George: Anna, honey, I think you'd better start letting go of her.

Anna: You think so? I just want to keep her from getting hurt.

George: People have to make their own mistakes, Anna. You've been a good mother and set a good example. That's all you can do. Now. What's for dinner?

Anna: Stew.

George: Again?

Anna: Now that's another thing. George, I do the best I can. The prices in the supermarket go up every week. We can't have steak the way we used to. I wish the President would do something about this inflation. Soon we'll be having soup for dinner.

George: I suppose I could take a second job.

Anna: Then we'd never see you, honey. It's bad enough as it is. We'll get by.

George: Why did you mention a transfer a moment ago?

Anna: Oh. I guess I was thinking about a little house somewhere.

George: "Little" houses are a lot of money these days. I thought you liked the apartment. And I know you like the neighborhood, and we have good neighbors. And . . . .

Anna: I know. You know, I was talking to Mrs. Torres earlier and they're thinking about buying a house in Carleton to be near their grandchildren. And I suppose Mr. Torres will be thinking about retire-

	ment soon.
George:	I'd like to get a house, too. I'm tired of paying rent to old Mr. Fein, but where are we going to get a down payment?
Anna:	How much do we need?
George:	It depends on a lot of things.
Anna:	Like what?
George:	It varies from bank to bank. Most banks ask for twenty to thirty percent. Sometimes more. But, Anna, are you sure you want to live in the suburbs? It might be lonely for Amanda. It might be harder for her to make friends.
Anna:	I don't know what to do. You know that nice little Cynthia Miles from church? Amanda doesn't like her anymore because she says she's boring.
George:	She probably is.
Anna:	There you go again. I don't want her to have the wrong friends. You know how the schools are. And next year she'll be in high school. As for the neighborhood kids . . . they're dying on our very own roof. And there's nothing we can do about it.
George:	There are private schools.

Anna:	How can we afford a private school? They cost almost $4,000.00 a year.
George:	Well, what do you want me to do?
Anna:	I'm not blaming you, honey. Why don't you talk to Mr. Torres? He's figured it out.
George:	Don't bug me, Anna. I've got to think about it.
Anna:	I invited them over for coffee after dinner.
George:	You what?
Anna:	They're coming over.
George:	I wish you'd asked me first. I was looking forward to some peace and quiet tonight.
Anna:	I thought . . . .
George:	You thought. You think too much. Well, it's all right. We'll see what Carlos has to say.
Anna:	I'm sorry, George.
George:	Hmmmm.

CULTURAL NOTES

1. In many families in the U.S., both the husband and the wife work. Some women work because they want to and others work because they have to. Traditionally, women stayed home and took care of the house and children. Today, many women go back to work as soon as the children begin school. Some return to work a month after their baby is born.

   In this chapter, George asks Anna about how she would feel if he got a transfer and they had to move. Anna is not worried because she feels that she can get another job easily. Even though many women have careers and some have important jobs, some women, like Anna, feel that their husbands' jobs are more important than theirs.
   - *Do you think Anna is right?*

2. Americans believe people should be independent. We respect people who can take care of themselves and make their own decisions. We want our children to be independent, but we want to be close to them, too. Often we are not sure at what age to "let them go" and permit our children to make all their own decisions. Anna has this problem with Amanda.
   - *Do people in your country value independence as much as Americans do?*

3. For most American families, an important part of the "American Dream" is owning a house. With the average price of a single family house over $60,000 and rising rapidly, it is becoming more and more difficult every year to make the dream come true.
   - *Would you like to own your own home someday?*

COMPREHENSION EXERCISES
Face the Facts

If the sentence is true, write "T." If the sentence is false, write "F."

1. ___ Amanda likes the way the man in 5W looks.

2. ___ The Post Office must give a promotion to the man who has the highest scores on a test.

3. ___ George thinks that Anna is a good mother.

4. ___ The Fieldings are going to have steak for dinner.

5. ___ The Fieldings have enough money for a down payment on a house.

Read Between the Lines

If, in your opinion, the sentence is true, write "T." If, in your opinion, the sentence is false, write "F." Make an inference.

1. ___ Anna doesn't want Amanda to get involved with Willie Dorio.

2. ___ Anna wishes that she could spend more time with her family.

3. ___ Anna is worried that Amanda will be hurt by prejudice because she is black.

4. ___ George is happy that Anna invited Mr. and Mrs. Torres over for coffee.

MORE DIFFICULT COMPREHENSION EXERCISES

Find the Supporting Details

1. Anna Fielding is worried about her daughter for a number of reasons. Write some of them here:

   becuse her daugher is late from school.
   2 becuse her daugher knows wrong friends

2. George Fielding is not sure that having a house is a good idea. Write two of his worries here:

   They don't have enough money
   2 Amanda may be harder for

Make a Judgment

What is your opinion of Anna as a mother? Do you agree with George that she has been a good one? Discuss your opinion and your reasons for it with your classmates.

VOCABULARY EXERCISES

Mind Your Words

be involved with

bug (v.)

gorgeous

Look at the following exercises. They will help you understand how the items are used. You may use your dictionary to find their definitions. Remember, we are working with the meanings of the items as they appear in the dialogue; they may have other meanings in other contexts.

BE INVOLVED WITH

"He's *involved with* the boy who got murdered on the roof, you know."

Another way to say "he's involved with" as used in the example above is:

1. he knows
2. he was in the same place as
3. he has a relationship with

According to the definition above, which sentence uses *be involved with* correctly?

1. He's involved with the television.
2. He's involved with a girl from Germany.

3. He's involved with a movie he just saw.
4. He's involved with hanging up the phone.
5. He's involved with a new pair of shoes.

BUG (used as a verb)
"Don't *bug* me, Anna."

A good synonym for *bug* is:

1. bother
2. hurt
3. help

Look up the word *bug* in your dictionary. As used in the example above, *bug* is slang. Mr. Fielding would probably not use the word *bug* when talking to:

1. Amanda
2. Willie
3. his boss
4. Mrs. Gold

When George says, "Don't bug me, Anna," he means:

1. Anna mentioned the subject (of buying a house) *once* before.
2. Anna has never mentioned the subject before.
3. Anna talks about the subject a lot.

GORGEOUS

"Oh, Mom, did you see that *gorgeous* new man in 5W?"

The word *gorgeous* in this sentence is:
1. positive
2. negative
3. neutral

Look up the word *gorgeous* in the dictionary. Which of the following definitions does *not* mean the same as *gorgeous* in the sentence above?
(1.) brilliantly colored
2. handsome
(3.) wonderful

When Amanda uses the word *gorgeous,* she is being:
1. scientific
2. medical
3. careful
(4.) emotional

True or False: Women use the word *gorgeous* more often than men.

THE FACTS OF LIFE

Buying a House

This chapter's Facts of Life is about the problems and costs of buying a house. Some people want to have a house someday. Others don't. If the topic interests you read on. If not, you might want to work on something else.

A house is the most expensive thing most people will ever buy. Very few people have enough money of their own to buy a home, so they have to borrow money from a bank. Borrowing from a bank to buy a house is called "taking a mortgage." The bank usually lends money or gives a mortgage, for twenty-five years. This means that the person who borrows has twenty-five years to pay back the money. The bank lends this money with interest, and the borrower makes equal monthly payments to the bank until he has paid the mortgage. Houses are so expensive that many people nowadays have to borrow as much as $50,000. In other words, they will have a $50,000 mortgage.

How can you get a mortgage? When you find a house you like, you go to a bank—sometimes it is necessary to go to a few banks—and apply for one. The bank will investigate you and decide if they think you are a good risk. They will want to know what kind of job you have, what kind of salary you make, and how long you have had the job. They will also want to know how much money you have.

In addition, the banks will require a down payment. Depending on which state you live in, the bank may require as much as 30% of the price of the house as a down payment. The bank will then lend you the rest of the money to buy the house. Many people are never able to buy a house because they can not save enough money for the down payment. Look at this example:

The house you want to buy costs $70,000.

The bank tells you that you have to give them a 30% down payment.

$$\begin{array}{r} \$70,000 \\ .30 \\ \hline \$21,000.00 \end{array}$$

You will have to give the bank $21,000.

$$\begin{array}{r} \$70,000 \\ -21,000 \\ \hline \$49,000 \end{array}$$

You will need at least a $49,000 mortgage. If you borrow $50,000 for twenty-five years and the bank wants 9½% interest, your monthly payment will be $436.85. After twenty-five years you will have returned a total of $131,055 to the bank.

If you borrow $50,000 for thirty years at the same interest, your monthly payment will be $420.43. After thirty years, you will have returned $151,355 to the bank.

Unfortunately, there are still more costs in buying a house. These are called *closing costs*. Some of these are:

1. your lawyer
   (You have to have a lawyer to make sure everything is legal.)
2. the bank's lawyer
   (You have to pay for him to prepare all the documents and the mortgage, etc.)
3. state and local fees
   (You have to pay to record the change of owners.)
4. title insurance fee
   (This pays for an investigation to make sure that the person who is selling the house owns it completely.)
5. property inspection
   (You will want to hire an engineer to check

that the wood, the pipes, electricity, and heating system are in good condition.)

6. extra costs

(The people who are selling sometimes want you to buy the carpets, the curtains or their refrigerator.)

A word to the wise: banks and lawyers are like everybody else. They want to make money. Before you choose a bank or a lawyer, shop around. The differences in fees and interest rates among banks and lawyers will surprise you. You might save a lot of money.

Before you buy a house, here are some things you might think about.

1. What are the taxes on the house? Taxes and tax rates differ enormously from place to place and state to state. Homeowners have to pay taxes in addition to paying the mortgage. Houses are sometimes more expensive in towns with *low* taxes. Towns with low taxes often have more factories.

2. What are the schools like? Do they have good or bad reputations? The value of a house may be higher or lower depending on the quality of the school district.

3. Most houses are sold through real estate agents. When people decide what area they want to live in, they find a real estate agent in that area. The agent will then show the customer the houses he has been asked to sell. There is a fee for the agent's services but it is paid by the seller, not the buyer. Nevertheless, the cost is passed along to the buyer. If you can buy a house directly from the owner you would probably save some money. (The agent's commission can be as high as 6 or 8% of the cost of the house. On a $70,000 house, you might be able to save $4,000.)

4. In general, in the United States, prices are fixed. However, we bargain when we buy a used car, when we buy old things, and when we buy a house. It is difficult to say what a house is worth. Owners usually say the price they would like to get, then they add a little for the agent's commission. This is called the "asking price." If they do not want to bargain (they have plenty of time to sell), they will tell you that their price is "firm."

Here are some real estate ads. Take a look at them and the abbreviations.

| 1. BAY CITY HTS-1 fam det, 6 rms, mod elect kitch-dish-wshr-mod bth-long yard w/ drvwy-$47,500   555-4146 |

Abbreviations:
fam = family
det = detached

rms = rooms
mod = modern
elect = electric
kitch = kitchen
dishwshr = dishwasher
bth = bathroom
w/ = with
drvwy = driveway

2.

MONROE
When Edward was king our spacious Jefferson area home was young! Asking $88,000, with quick poss. avail.
GILL & McREADY, INC
Realtors   555-6201

Abbreviations:
poss. = possession
avail. = available

3.

NEWTOWN. 3 BR split level ½ acre on quiet cul de sac, LR, formal DR, eat-in kitch, fam rm, encl porch, WW carpet, cent A/C, alum siding, mid $80's. Owner 555-6149

Abbreviations:
BR = bedroom
LR = living room
DR = dining room
encl = enclosed
WW = wall-to-wall
cent A/C = central air conditioning
alum = aluminum

4.

LAKESIDE PARK. Immac 6 rms, 2½ yr Col. 1½ bths, w/w crptg, a must see at $59,000.
Lakeside Park Realty, Realtors
Member Network of Homes.
555-7740

Abbreviations:
Immac = immaculate
Col = colonial
w/w = wall-to-wall
carptg = carpeting

5.

Seaview Carriage Hse
1 block ocean, 5 bdr, 2½ bth, 100x150 lot, fplc, new kitch, greenhse, attchd garage, liv rm, din rm, w/w crpt, master bdr 24x30, brkfst area. By owner.
Princ only. Asking $92,500.
555-5043

Abbreviations:
Hse = house
bdr = bedroom
fplc = fireplace
greenhse = greenhouse
attchd = attached
brkfst = breakfast
liv = living
din = dining
princ = principals (buyers)

6.

MORGANTOWN By owner re-locating, Colonial year round or summer home. 1st flr LR, DR, den, kit, plyrm, 2nd 4 BR, bth. Natural oak woodwork, full attic insul, HWH, new wiring, steel siding, exceptional view
$36,000.   555-3434

Abbreviations:
flr = floor
kit = kitchen
plyrm = playroom
insul = insulation
HWH = hot water heater

7.

SPAIN
Villa overlookg Mediterranean 3 BR, 2½ bths. 1¼ hrs from Malaga Int'l Airport.
Call Judy Lawrence,
LAWRENCE & LAWRENCE
555-0659

Abbreviations:
overlookg = overlooking
Int'l = international
hrs = hours

8.

```
         SOUTH MEADOW
   REDUCED OVER $12,000!
   Originally $98,000—NOW
   $85,900 for exciting Contem-
   porary Split! Bright, large
   rooms. Cathedral ceilings. 3-4
   bedrms, 2½ bths. Many extras
   incl ctrl air, wet bar, patio,
   deck! Must be sold—hurry!
   Excl Agt.
   VANGUARD        555-5108
```

Abbreviations:
  incl = including
  ctrl air = central air conditioning
  excl agt = exclusive agent (This house is available
       only by contacting this agent.)

9.

```
         EASTBURY
         CHALET
        Excellent View
   20 Minutes from 3 Ski Areas
   3 Bedrooms, Living Room
   with dining area, kitchen w/
   refrig & stove, 1½ bths, wrap-
   around deck, Franklin stove,
   rugs & drapes.
        $55,000 firm.
        Dys 555-5158
        Eves 555-7496
```

Abbreviations:
  w/refrig = with
       refrigerator
  dys = days
  eves = evenings

10.

```
   GREECE-Island of Rhodes
   2 story country hse, 3BRs,
   livrm, patio, utils etc situated
   on 1500 sq mtr plt 5 min wlk fr
   beaut sandy bch, $100,000
   Write to:
     Constantine Papogapolos,
   8 Nike Street, Athens, Greece
```

Abbreviations:
  livrm = living room
  utils = utilities
  sq mtr = square meter
  plt = plot
  min = minutes

  wlk = walk
  fr = from
  beaut = beautiful
  bch = beach

EXERCISES

1. Which of these ads were placed by the owners and which by agencies/agents?
2. Which of these ads has a firm price?
3. Some of these ads give you a lot of information. Some give almost none. Compare ad #1 with ad #2. What is the real purpose of ad #1?
4. Would you like to buy any of these houses? Which one(s)? Explain why.

See supplementary exercises on pages 153 and 163.

Some questions you might like to discuss with your classmates:

Do you like people to give you advice?
Do you listen to advice and follow it? Or do you prefer to "live and learn" from your own experiences?

Do you think it is all right to ask your friends for favors? For example, if they work for a company that makes bags, would you ask your friend to get you a bag at a low price?

Say these words

after your teacher or after an American friend.

ad·vice′	deal	fa′·vor	re·ceiv′·er	ser′·vice
ap·point′·ment	de·live′·ry	im·ma·ture′	(telephone)	sis′·ter·ly
char′·ac·ter	des′·per·ate	mind (n.)	san′·dal	size
				un·til′

phrases

ask (*someone*) out
be too much
get a·way′ with (*something*)
get to·geth′·er
get off
hang up
 have (*something*) in mind

have a hard time of
 (*something*)
hold (*possessive*) breath
I take it . . . .
(*possessive*) old man
a one-track mind
put a·side′

show (*someone*) a good time
So long.
stop in
Why not . . . ?
You're too much.

In this chapter, Sally gets to know more about Willie.

As you read think about these questions:

Why doesn't Willie want to talk to Sally on the phone?
Does Sally ask for her sister's advice about Willie?
Who is Roberta?
Is Sally dating a lot of men?
How did Willie get his job at Pretty Feet?

A FRIEND INDEED

(Sally picks up the phone and dials Willie's number.)
Willie: Hello.
Sally: Hello, Willie? This is Sally. What are you doing?
Willie: Hi, Nate. How are you doing?

Sally: It's not Nate. It's me, Sally.
Willie: Yeah, I know. Look, Nate, I'm tied up right now. Why don't we get together tomorrow night, okay? I'll call you. So long.

(He hangs up. Sally looks up at the receiver trying to figure out what's just happened. Then she smiles to herself.)

Sally: What a character!
Emily: Who?
Sally: Willie.
Emily: He's a bit immature, isn't he?
Sally: Maybe, but I like him anyway. He's had a hard time of it.
Emily: Are you thinking about seeing him again?

Sally: Sure. Why not?

Emily: He's not exactly your type.

Sally: What is my type? Listen, he's a friend. That's all. Besides he's not bad-looking, either.

Emily: What does he think of that?

Sally: What?

Emily: That he's your friend.

Sally: I don't think it's what he had in mind.

Emily: I'll bet. When are you going to see him?

Sally: Tomorrow.

Emily: Sally . . . .

Sally: Listen, Emily. Do me a favor—just don't give me any advice. I know what I'm doing.

Emily: Okay. If you say so.

(The next day, back at the same coffeehouse on 86th Street)

Willie: Well, when are we going to the disco?

Sally: Soon.

Willie: Well, I won't hold my breath. Oh, hey, about last night . . . .

Sally: I take it you had company. What was her name?

Willie: Uh . . . Roberta, I think.

Sally: You *think*?

Willie: Yeah. Roberta. I met her at a party.

Sally: What was she like?

Willie: Not bad. Kind of dumb, but good-looking.

Sally: I wonder what she thought of you.

Willie: I don't know. I didn't ask. I showed her a good time.

Sally: I can't believe that you get away with it.

Willie: Some have it, and some don't. And who have you been going out with lately?

Sally: Well, the guy who interviewed me for a job last Thursday asked me out.

Willie: Did you go?

Sally: No.

Willie: I'll bet you didn't get the job, either.

Sally: You're right. I didn't.

Willie: Why didn't you go out with him?

Sally: Number one: I'm not that desperate for a job. And number two: I think he was married.

Willie: You're too much. You really are.

Sally: Oh, by the way, did you call that job counseling service?

Willie: Yeah. They're very busy. I couldn't get an appointment until next month.

Sally: Really?

Willie: Yeah. And they're expensive, too.

Sally: How much?

Willie: One hundred fifty dollars.

Sally: That much?

Willie: Yeah. You know, I've been doing a lot of thinking.

Sally: Don't tell me! Willie, the Lover of 88th Street, *thinks*!

Willie: What do you mean by that?

Sally: I'm just kidding, Willie. Go on.

Willie: You started me on this. It's all your fault. You know, I could run that shoe store. I could run it better than the jerk that manages it now.

Sally: I'm sure you could. How did you get that job in the first place?

Willie: My old man drives a shoe delivery truck and heard about the job. He does favors for them, so they did a favor for him.

Sally: It's all in who you know, isn't it?

Willie: Yeah, in a way. But, now they're the lucky ones. I'm their best salesman.

Sally: There's a lot of money in sales.

Willie: Not at Pretty Feet.

Sally: You can sell other things besides shoes.

Willie: I guess so. I could also be the manager. Hey! We're having a sale. Why don't you stop in tomorrow? I'll give you a good deal.

Sally: Thanks. I will. I need a pair of sandals for summer.

Willie: Sure. What size do you take?

Sally: 7½. When do you close?

Willie: Tomorrow? Six o'clock. I'll put some sandals aside for you.

(Willie laughs.)

Sally: What are you laughing about?

Willie: At least I'll get your shoes off!

Sally: You have a one-track mind.

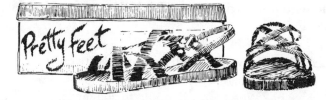

CULTURAL NOTES

1. Sally does not want to date someone who is in a position to offer her a job. We have an expression, "Don't mix business with pleasure." We try to keep our personal lives separate from our professional lives. Often workers at the same level will become friends outside of work. But usually we do not mix socially with people above us except at one or two parties a year.

2. Very often in the U.S., people get jobs in a company because someone in the company knows them. We call this "having connections." Many people from foreign countries got their first jobs in the U.S. through friends. If you are looking for a job, don't be afraid to use your connections. However, if you get a job through your connections, it is not a good idea to tell other people you work with about it. They might think you did not deserve the job.

COMPREHENSION EXERCISES

Face the Facts

If the sentence is true, write "T." If the sentence is false, write "F."

1. ___ Willie knows it is Sally and not Nate on the phone.

2. ___ Emily doesn't think Willie is right for Sally.

3. ___ Sally is not going to see Willie for a few days.

4. ___ Sally has not been able to get any job interviews.

5. ___ Willie wants to get a new job because he's not a good salesman.

Read Between the Lines

If the sentence is true, write "T." If the sentence is false, write "F." Make an inference.

1. ___ Sally thinks Willie treats girls very well.

2. ___ Willie thinks he treats girls well.

3. ___ Willie thinks Sally didn't get the job because she didn't go out with the interviewer.

4. ___ $150.00 isn't very much money to Willie.

5. ___ Willie thinks he could do a better job than his boss at Pretty Feet.

MORE DIFFICULT COMPREHENSION EXERCISES

Find the Supporting Details

Sally and Willie help each other in a number of ways. List as many as you can here:

_____

_____

_____

_____

Make a Judgment

1. Willie, like all people, has good qualities and bad qualities. Look at the information in this story and list his good points and then his bad ones.

Good Points	Bad Points
_____	_____
_____	_____
_____	_____

2. If you were the owner of Pretty Feet, would you make Willie the store manager? Why or why not?
3. Emily doesn't want Sally to go out with Willie. How strongly does she feel about it? What do you think she should do?

VOCABULARY EXERCISES
Mind Your Words

character

I take it
tied up

Look at the following exercises. They will help you understand how these items are used. You may use your dictionary to find their definitions. Remember, we are working with the meanings of the items as they appear in the dialogue; they may have other meanings in other contexts.

CHARACTER
"What a *character!*"

Look up the word *character* in the dictionary. As you see, *character* has many meanings.

When we talk about a *character* as used in the example above, the person we are talking about is probably:
1. interesting
2. a little strange
3. ordinary
4. unpleasant

Another way to say *What a character!* is:
1. What a famous or important person!
2. What a strange or unusual person!
3. What a literary or musical person!

I TAKE IT
"*I take it* you had company."

How many of the following could you substitute for *I take it* as used in the example above?
1. I guess
2. I'm sure
3. I imagine
4. I know

When Sally says, *I take it you had company,* she is:
1. 100% sure
2. 95% sure
3. 50% sure
4. 25% sure

that Willie was with someone else.

Which of the following pairs of sentences show that the speaker has a reason to say, *I take it?*
1. I take it you like your job. You work five days a week.
2. I take it you've been sick. You look pale.

3. I take it you are rich. You work five days a week.
4. I take it you like that shirt. You wear it almost every day.
5. I take it you've been sick. I was sick last month.

TIED UP
"I'm *tied up* right now."

Instead of saying *I'm tied up*, Willie could have said:
1. I'm busy
2. I'm a prisoner
3. I'm tired

I'm tied up is a nice way to say that you can't talk to or see someone. It's a popular phrase in business and industry. It is an excuse, but it doesn't give any reasons. Therefore, you probably should not use it with:
1. your wife
2. your boss
3. your friends
4. your children

THE FACTS OF LIFE
More About Job Interviews

In this chapter, we found out that during an interview Sally's interviewer asked her out. This was something that no interviewer should do, and Sally was probably quite correct to refuse. Because of certain Federal Laws, there are a number of things that an interviewer is not supposed to ask you. Some of these things are:

1. It's illegal to ask personal questions about your age, height, weight, strength, and physical appearance. The interviewer can notice these things before you are hired and she or he can ask you questions about them *after* you are hired if there is a specific reason for asking them (For example, some companies must know your age for health insurance, etc.)
2. It's illegal to ask personal questions about your marital status and children. The interviewer cannot ask you if you are married, engaged, living with anyone, or any similar questions.
3. It's illegal to ask questions about where you live or any other questions about what you have or don't have.
4. It's illegal to ask questions about your military record or criminal record. You can be asked if you were in the military; but you cannot be asked if you served in the Army, Navy, or any other kind of specific information. No questions about whether you have ever been arrested or have been in jail are supposed to be asked. If the job involves security, the company can do a security check on you after

they have told you that they would like to hire you. What can you do if the interviewer asks you one or more of these questions? Most people we have talked with suggest that you answer the question. You might want to let the interviewer know (very carefully) that you know that she or he is not supposed to ask such questions. Ask your teacher or an American friend for suggestions on what you can say in an interview. If it upsets you that the interviewer has made a number of unprofessional comments and asked a number of illegal questions, you can call the Equal Employment Opportunity Commission office and complain. Their number should be listed in your phone book.

EXERCISES

1. Working in small groups, make a list of some questions that interviewers are *not* supposed to ask. (For example: How old are you? Have you ever been arrested?)
2. Select a few of the questions you made in exercise 1 and think of some responses you might give. You might want to answer the question; you might want to make a humorous response; or you might want to answer the question with a question of your own.

See supplementary exercises on page 155.

One of the topics in this chapter is racial prejudice. If you do not want to discuss this topic in class, please don't feel that you have to. We have included it because it is of great concern to many people. We feel that this topic cannot be avoided.

Almost everyone has prejudices. There are things that we like and do not like, and we often feel very strongly about them.

Some questions you might want to discuss with your classmates:

What are some of the things you are prejudiced against? If you want to, share them with your classmates.

What things are other people prejudiced against?

Is there prejudice in your country? Against what? Against whom?

Few people are lucky enough to go through life and say that no one has ever discriminated against them. Have you ever felt that you were looked down on because of your nationality, ethnicity, race, age, religion, or sex? If you want to, describe an experience to your classmates.

Say these words

after your teacher or after an American friend.

an'·gel	mess	toast (v.)	Shame on
a·shamed'	of·fense'		(_someone_).
beg	o'·ther·wise	_phrases_	
bran'·dy	pour	be cra′·zy	
con·si'·der	pre'·cious	about	
dia'·mond	pre'·ju·dice	help out	
em·bar'·rass	re·vol·u'·tion	look (_some-_	
for'·eign	shock	_one_) straight	
glass	skin	in the eye	
in·sin·cere'	spare (v.)	see the	
in·tend'	sub'·urbs	hand'·writ·ing	
in·vite'	tease	on the wall	

In this chapter the Torreses and the Fieldings talk about themselves and their feelings.

As you read, think about these questions:

Why is George worried about moving to a white suburb?
What happened to the Mirandas' daughter?
Why were the Mirandas luckier than the Torreses?
How do neighbors often act in American suburbs?
Why is Pilar upset about her oldest daughter?

KNOWING THE SCORE

(The Torreses and the Fieldings are sitting around the table in the Fieldings' kitchen, having coffee and cake.)

Anna: What do you know about that new young man on the top floor?

Mrs. Torres: Mrs. Gold likes him, and so does Sally.

Anna: Sally is a lovely girl.

George: She sure is!

Anna: Shame on you, George. You're old enough to be her father.

George: I'm just teasing.

Pilar: Clara is crazy about him. She plans her afternoons so she can meet him when he comes home from work.

Anna: Really? My Amanda is crazy about him, too. She thinks he's "dreamy."

Pilar: So Clara isn't the only one. *(They laugh.)*

Anna: You know, to change the subject for a moment, ever since you mentioned that you were looking for a house, I haven't been able to think about anything else. I guess I've always dreamed about living in a house in the suburbs someday.

George: But we're not sure about moving to a white suburb.

Pilar: I know what you mean. We have friends, the Mirandas, who live in Mortentown. We've known them for . . . oh . . . I guess it's about thirty years.

Carlos: Watch out, Pilar. You're giving away your age.

George: She doesn't look a day over twenty-one.

Pilar: Oh, come on. Be serious. Felipe and Consuela, our friends, left Cuba before we did. Felipe saw the handwriting on the wall.

Carlos: You've got to give him credit for that.

Pilar: They sold everything they had and bought diamonds.

Carlos: Everyone thought they were crazy.

Pilar: We all thought they were crazy to want to leave. A lot of us were in favor of the revolution.

Carlos: We thought that things would change for the better.

Pilar: Anyway, they left in the early days when you could take things with you. They begged us to

	go with them, but we didn't want to give up our friends, our country, and all that we had.
Carlos:	It was the biggest mistake of my life.
Pilar:	When they got here, they sold the diamonds and opened a small business. They've done very well. Three years ago they were able to buy a nice house out in Mortentown.
	Now, to get to your point, George—one day their daughter, Linda, came home from school. She was in the first grade. She looked very upset but she wouldn't tell her mother what it was. When Felipe got home, he asked Linda why she was upset.
Carlos:	*Pobrecita.*
Pilar:	"Daddy, am I different?" she asked him. He asked her what she meant.
George:	I know what she meant.
Pilar:	She said that the other children at school said that her father was black. She said, "Daddy, is it true? Am I black, too?" Felipe didn't know where to begin.
Anna:	I remember the day that Amanda found out she was black.
Pilar:	Well, I suppose that it's true. Felipe *is* very dark. But Linda was just a little girl. She had never thought about skin color before.
George:	You mean that you don't think about color in Cuba?
Carlos:	I can't say that we don't. Some do. But it's a

	shock to be called black in the U.S. We're not black. We're Cuban.
George:	Oh?
Carlos:	Hey, listen, no offense intended. You're our friends, and you're black. Color doesn't matter to us. You're our friends, that's all.
Pilar:	Do you understand? To us it seems wrong to think of Felipe as black. He's Cuban.
George:	Sure. It's not easy to be black in America.
Pilar:	It isn't easy to be foreign in America, either.
Anna:	Well, but things are changing a bit. Twenty years ago we could not have even considered buying a house in the suburbs. No one would have sold us one. You know, we're not ashamed to be black. We can look anyone straight in the eye. We're a hard-working, God-fearing family.
George:	Listen, I don't give a damn what people think as long as they don't mess with our lives.
Carlos:	I feel the same way.
Pilar:	I wonder if we're doing the right thing wanting to move. We don't want to go where we're not wanted. Everybody seems friendly and polite. Neighbors smile and say hello, but they don't invite you into their homes. I don't know how to explain it . . . they're insincere. They tell you they'd like to see you, but then they never call. They're always busy. They'll help you out if you're in trouble, but, other-

	wise, they want to be left alone. Why are they like that? I don't know what to think about Americans, sometimes.
George:	*We're* Americans.
Pilar:	Yes, and we're lucky to have you as friends. But other Americans seem different. At first I thought something was wrong with me. Then I thought it was prejudice against foreigners. Now I think it's just the way Americans are. But I don't like it.
Anna:	Your oldest daughter married an American, didn't she?
Pilar:	Yes, and now she's like the rest of them. I don't like that either. I have to call her to ask if we can come over. Imagine that! Call your own daughter!
George:	That's the way it is here, Pilar.
Pilar:	It was never this way back home. A mother doesn't call her own daughter and ask her if she can spare a few minutes of her precious time. My door was always open to my mother. I loved her . . . it . . . we . . . .(*Mrs. Torres covers her face with her hands and begins to cry.*)
Carlos:	Pilar. My little Pilar. That was many years ago. Don't cry. Don't cry, my angel, you'll embarrass the Fieldings.
Pilar:	(*to the Fieldings*) I'm sorry.

Anna:	(*to Pilar*) Have another cup of coffee, Pilar honey.
George:	How about a drink, Pilar? Maybe a little brandy.
Pilar:	I shouldn't.
Carlos:	Go ahead.
Pilar:	Well, maybe a little.
George:	Carlos?
Carlos:	Sure. A good idea.

(*George gets the brandy and pours four glasses.*)

George:	How about a toast? To the future. It's got to be better.

1. Our neighbors are often just the people who live near us. We do not have to meet with them socially or become friends. This does not mean that neighbors do not talk; it just means that they are not good friends.
   - *Is it the same in your country?*

2. If you want to visit someone, it is always a good idea to call first and ask if you can. When you invite someone to your house or to go out, give the invitation about one week in advance. If you're having a party or inviting people to go out on a holiday, invite people two or three weeks in advance.
   - *Do you think this is also necessary for close friends?*

3. Americans often appear insincere to people from other countries because we say things that sound like invitations, but are really just ways of saying we like you.
   "Let's have lunch sometime."
   "We must get together again soon."
   When we make a real invitation, we will almost always mention a specific time.
   "Let's have lunch *on Tuesday*."
   "We must get together again soon. Would you like to come to a party we're having in *two weeks*?"
   - *Have you felt that Americans are insincere? Why?*

COMPREHENSION EXERCISES
Face the Facts

If the sentence is true, write "T." If the sentence is false, write "F."

1. ___ Anna Fielding wants to live in a house in the suburbs.

2. ___ Pilar is less than thirty years old.

3. ___ Felipe and Consuela Miranda brought most of their possessions with them to the U.S.

4. ___ Carlos identifies himself by his native country, not by his skin color.

5. ___ Pilar understands and likes the American way of life very much.

Read Between the Lines

If the sentence is true, write "T." If the sentence is false, write "F." Make an inference.

1. ___ Carlos does not understand why his daughter is crazy about Willie.

2. ___ There is no prejudice against blacks in Cuba.

3. ___ The Fieldings are worried about moving to the suburbs because the Fieldings are black and the suburbs are mostly white.

4. ___ George wants everyone to like him.

5. ___ Anna is proud of herself and her family.

MORE DIFFICULT COMPREHENSION EXERCISES
Find the Supporting Details

1. Pilar finds Americans difficult to understand. What are several things she finds confusing?

   _____

   _____

2. How has the Mirandas' life been different from the Torres'?

   _____

   _____

Make a Judgment

1. Do you think the Torreses are prejudiced against blacks? Discuss your opinion and your reason for it with your classmates.

2. Do you think Pilar's older, married daughter (Isabel) loves her mother? Discuss your opinion and your reasons for it with your classmates.

VOCABULARY EXERCISES

Mind Your Words

look (someone) straight in the eye
the handwriting on the wall

Look at the following exercises. They will help you understand how these phrases are used. You may use your dictionary to find their definitions. Remember, we are working with the meanings of the phrases as they appear in the dialogue; they may have other meanings in other contexts.

LOOK *SOMEONE* STRAIGHT IN THE EYE
"We can look anyone *straight in the eye.*"

When we talk to others, we make eye contact. If you don't look at me, when you talk to me, I will think you are being dishonest or that you have something to hide. When an American parent disciplines his child, he will say, "Look at me when I talk to you." We assume that you are not paying attention if you don't look at us when we talk. This rule, making eye contact, applies to all people; men, women, children, rich, and poor.

Which of the following are probably true when George Fielding says, *"We can look anyone straight in the eye"*?
1. His family has nothing to hide.
2. He and his wife are proud of being honest, hard-working citizens.
3. He and his family are angry at other people so they keep an eye on them.
4. They don't have any respect for their superiors so they refuse to keep their eyes down.

In which of the following situations is it *especially* important to look the other person in the eye when you are listening or speaking to them?
1. At the clerk when you are buying meat in the grocery store
2. At the interviewer when you are having a job interview
3. At other drivers while you are driving a car
4. At the police when you are explaining why you did something
5. At your teachers when you are telling them why you couldn't do your homework

THE HANDWRITING ON THE WALL
"Felipe saw *the handwriting on the wall.*"

The handwriting on the wall is a phrase from the Bible (Daniel:5). It refers to predicting that something will happen in the future. In the story, Mr. Torres says that when there was a revolution in Cuba, his friend saw *the handwriting on the wall* and left the country. If the company you work for is having financial problems, you can say that you see *the handwriting on the wall* and start looking for another job.

Look at the following situations. What would *the handwriting on the wall* tell the person to do?

Example: I can't find a job, and I've been looking for six months. *The handwriting is on the wall. I'd better get some help from a job counselor.*

(Please note: Many different answers are possible, so please share your opinions with your classmates.)

1. The car has been difficult to start all week. The

   handwriting is on the wall. I'd better _____

   _____

2. Glen and his wife don't talk to each other very much anymore. _____

   _____

3. After she runs upstairs to her apartment, Karen starts coughing and doesn't stop for about five minutes.

   _____

   _____

4. One of my back teeth has been aching off and on for about three weeks. _____

   _____

5. The roof leaks. The water is dirty. The ceiling is falling down. There's no heat, and it's cold outside.

   _____

   _____

THE FACTS OF LIFE
The Bill of Rights

A special vocabulary is often needed to read and understand the law. For that reason, you will probably find this chapter's Facts of Life material difficult. But the Constitution is probably the most important document in American history. So . . . .

The first ten amendments to the Constitution are called the Bill of Rights. These and Amendments number 14, 15, and 19 are what Americans consider basic rights.

Here are some of the Amendments that are most important in protecting our civil rights.

AMENDMENT [I]

Congress shall make no law respecting an establishment of religion, or prohibiting the free exercise thereof; or abridging the freedom of speech, or of the press; or the right of the people peaceably to assemble, and to petition the Government for a redress of grievances.

AMENDMENT [II]

A well regulated Militia, being necessary to the security of a free State, the right of the people to keep and bear Arms, shall not be infringed.

AMENDMENT [IV]

The right of the people to be secure in their persons, houses, papers, and effects, against unreasonable searches and seizures, shall not be violated, and no Warrants shall issue, but upon probable cause, supported by Oath or affirmation, and particularly describing the place to be searched, and the persons or things to be seized.

AMENDMENT [V]

No person shall be held to answer for a capital, or otherwise infamous crime, unless on a presentment or indictment of a Grand Jury, except in cases arising in the land or naval forces, or in the Militia, when in actual service in time of War or public danger; nor shall any person be subject for the same offence to be twice put in jeopardy of life or limb; nor shall be compelled in any criminal case to be a witness against himself, nor be deprived of life, liberty, or property, without due process of law; nor shall private property be taken for public use, without just compensation.

AMENDMENT [VI]

In all criminal prosecutions, the accused shall enjoy the right to a speedy and public trial, by an impartial jury of the State and district wherein the crime shall have been committed, which district shall have been previously ascertained by law, and to be informed of the nature and cause of the accusation; to be confronted with the witnesses against him; to have compulsory process for obtaining witnesses in his favor, and to have the Assistance of Counsel for his defence.

AMENDMENT [VII]

In Suits at common law, where the value in controversy shall exceed twenty dollars, the right of trial by jury shall be preserved, and no fact tried by a jury, shall be otherwise re-examined in any Court of the United States, than according to the rules of the common law.

AMENDMENT [VIII]

Excessive bail shall not be required, nor excessive fines imposed, nor cruel and unusual punishments inflicted.

AMENDMENT [XIV]

Section 1. All persons born or naturalized in the United States, and subject to the jurisdiction thereof, are citizens of the United States and of the State wherein they reside. No State shall make or enforce any law which shall abridge the privileges or immunities of citizens of the United States; nor shall any State deprive any person of life, liberty, or property, without due process of law; nor deny to any person within its jurisdiction the equal protection of the laws.

AMENDMENT [XV]

Section 1. The right of citizens of the United States to vote shall not be denied or abridged by the United States or by any State on account of race, color, or previous condition of servitude.

Section 2. The Congress shall have power to enforce this article by appropriate legislation.

AMENDMENT [XIX]

The right of citizens of the United States to vote shall not be denied or abridged by the United States or by any State on account of sex.

Congress shall have power to enforce this article by appropriate legislation.

EXERCISES

1. Working in small groups, read the Amendments and select the right from the list that each Amendment protects.

   Note: Some Amendments protect more than one right.

   Example: The right to have and carry weapons.
   Amendment _____

   1. The right to have a public trial.
      Amendment _____

   2. The right to remain silent.
      Amendment _____

   3. The right to belong to any religious group.
      Amendment _____

4. The right of any citizen to vote.

Amendment _____

Amendment _____

b. the right of peaceful assembly

c. the right to bear arms

5. The right to a reasonable punishment for a crime.

Amendment _____

d. protection against unlawful search and seizure

2. Some terms used in the Constitution are very famous. Ask your teacher, another student, or an American friend to explain them to you. Then write what you think they mean in the empty space here.

e. protection against double jeopardy

f. right to due process of law

a. freedom of speech

g. right to counsel

h. right to trial by jury

i. protection against cruel and unusual punishment

See supplementary exercises on pages 155 and 164.

Some questions you might like to discuss with your classmates:

Have you ever had a noisy neighbor? What did you do?

In some countries parents decide who their children should marry and when they should marry. Do you think parents should arrange their children's marriages?

Say these words

after your teacher or after an American friend.

as′·pirin	ex·cuse′	mess (n.)	push
bath′·robe	faint (v.)	pack (v.)	quick′·ly
di′·a·ry	grab	pound (v.)	spe′·cial
di·vorce′	hon′·or	pre·serve′	stare (v.)
dou′·ble	junk	pur′·ple	swal′·low (v.)

phrases

be from the old count′·ry	E·nough′ is e·nough′.
be hard on *(someone)*	good house′·keep·ing
chick′·ens come home to roost	a·ward′
Damn it.	wake the dead
ei′·ther way	work out

In this story, you will find out why Willie left his parents' home and got an apartment.

As you read the story, think about these questions:

Why is Willie playing loud music at 1:30 in the morning?
Why didn't Willie want to marry the girl?
Why did Willie leave home?
Why did the girl's father just call Willie?
What does George think of Willie?

THE CHICKENS COME HOME TO ROOST

(It's late. You can hear loud music coming from Willie's apartment. George Fielding walks quickly up the stairs and knocks on Willie's door. There is no answer. He pounds on the door.)

George: *(shouting)* Open up, damn it!
Willie: *(shouting)* Okay, okay! I'm coming! Who is it?
George: George Fielding. 3W.
Willie: Hold on.

(Willie turns the music down and opens the door.)

George: Do you know what time it is?
Willie: Was the music too loud?
George: Was the music too loud? It could wake the dead. It's 1:30 in the morning, and you're keeping the whole building up. Enough is enough, kid.
Willie: Sorry. Really. I didn't know.

(Willie looks upset. The two men stand in the doorway in their bathrobes looking at each other.)

George: What's the matter, kid? Can't sleep?
Willie: It's a long story.
George: Want to talk about it? I mean, I'm up here now, and . . . .

(Willie looks at George for a minute.)

Willie: You want a drink?
George: Sure. What have you got?
Willie: Scotch.
George: Fine.
Willie: Sit down. I'll get it.

(George looks around for a place to sit.)

Willie: Over there. Just push that junk on the floor.
George: You don't get the good housekeeping award.

(Willie pours drinks.)

George: What's the story?
Willie: There was a girl at a place we used to go. She wasn't anything special. I hardly looked at her. One day my buddy tells me that this girl is crazy about me. She dreams about me. What am I supposed to do, right?

George: Uh huh . . . .

Willie: It's not my fault she dreams about me. She tells Nate's girl that she would do anything to have a date with me. She tells him, and he tells me. So one night I'm sitting around. Nothing's happening, so I ask her out. I figure why not. What have I got to lose? Right?

George: Uh huh . . . .

Willie: So I ask her out, and she's so happy she almost faints. I say, "How about a movie?" She says her parents are out. Why don't I come over there? Why not, right?

George: Mmmmmmmm . . . .

Willie: So I go over to her place. At first I don't know what to say. We talk about this and that. But then, what is there to say, you know?

George: Uh huh . . . .

Willie: Well, one thing leads to another—if you know what I mean.

George: Right.

Willie: So we had a good time, and so I see her again, right?

George: Right.

Willie: She's okay, you know. And she likes me, right?

George: Uh huh . . . .

Willie: But then she says she wants to get married. "Married?" I said. "Married? Are you crazy?" Then she starts to cry and tells me that she loves me and that she wants to marry me and that I'm the only guy she's ever loved.

George: Huh!

Willie: So I tell her she's crazy. I don't love her. I hardly even know her. And I won't marry her. I tell her I'll leave town first.

George: Kind of hard on her, weren't you?

Willie: That's not all. There's more. Her mother finds this diary she keeps. I don't know what she wrote in it, but the next thing I know, her father comes knocking on my door. He's from the old country, you know. He tells me I have to marry his daughter. I told him he was crazy, too. He turns purple and tells me I have to marry her.

George: Then what?

Willie: Next day her brother comes up to me on the way to work and grabs me by the shirt and tells me he'll kill me if I don't marry his sister. So I tell him he's dead if he tries.

George: Huh!

Willie: Then my mother starts crying day and night—her father tells my parents, right?

George: Terrific . . . .

Willie: My mother's crying all over the house. All of them tell me I have to marry her to preserve the honor of the families. What could I do? I went to my room, packed my stuff, called my buddy, Nate, and moved out. I stayed with him until I found this place. And here I am.

George: That's quite a story.

Willie: Yeah. That's what everyone says. But it gets worse.

George: It does?

Willie: Her father just called from the hospital.

George: The hospital? What happened?

Willie: She swallowed a bottle of aspirin.

George: Is she all right?

Willie: Yeah. I knew she was crazy, but, you know, swallowing aspirin . . . . Can you believe it?

George: So? What next?

Willie: Well, that's the thing. Her father wants me to go down there and see her.

George: How do you feel about that?

Willie: I suppose it wouldn't hurt, but . . . .

George: Uh . . . .

Willie: So, what do you think?

George: I don't know.

(Willie stares at the floor.)

George: Would you like another drink?

Willie: Yeah. Make mine a double.

COMPREHENSION EXERCISES

Face the Facts

If the sentence is true, write "T." If the sentence is false, write "F."

1. ___ Willie is a neat housekeeper.

2. ___ Willie loved the girl.

3. ___ Willie thinks the girl is crazy.

4. ___ Willie's parents don't want him to marry the girl.

5. ___ George doesn't know what to say to Willie about his problems.

Read Between the Lines

If the sentence is true, write "T." If the sentence is false, write "F." Make an inference.

1. ___ George Fielding is angry at Willie at the beginning of the chapter.

2. ___ Willie is playing the music loud because he's happy.

3. ___ Willie thinks the girl's problems are all her fault.

4. ___ George Fielding thinks Willie did the right thing in leaving home.

5. ___ George is angry at Willie at the end of the story.

MORE DIFFICULT COMPREHENSION EXERCISES

Find the Supporting Details

Willie is upset about his life for several reasons. Think of what you know about Willie from this chapter and from the others you have read. List as many reasons as you can to explain why he is upset.

_____

_____

Make a Judgment

1. Do you feel that Willie acted correctly? Should he marry the girl?
2. Do you feel that the girl acted correctly?
3. How does George feel about Willie's story? What would you have said in George's position?

VOCABULARY EXERCISES

Mind Your Words

a double
to turn purple

Look at the following exercises. They will help you understand how these phrases are used. You may use your dictionary to find their definitions. Remember, we are working with the meanings of the phrases as they appear in the dialogue: they may have other meanings in other contexts.

A DOUBLE
"Make mine *a double*."

In the example above, the word *mine* refers to:

1. a drink
2. George
3. a glass
4. an idea

The word *double* usually refers to:
1. quality
2. quantity or size
3. cost
4. importance

When Willie says, *Make mine a double,* he is probably referring to:
1. the quality of the drink
2. the cost of the drink
3. the kind of drink
4. the size of the drink

TO TURN PURPLE
"*He turns purple* and tells me I have to marry her."

To turn purple means:
1. to become very sad
2. to be very happy

3. to become very important
4. to get very angry

Colors have different meanings in different countries. In the example above, purple is the color of:

1. deep anger
2. a little sadness
3. great happiness
4. a little quietness

Below you will see two columns. Match the emotion or condition in column A to its color in column B. Do this exercise with other students or friends. If you can't match all the emotion to colors, ask an American to help you.

column A	column B
jealousy or envy	purple
anger (two colors)	black
fear or cowardice	
(two colors)	green
passion (two colors)	white
purity	yellow
death	red

Which of the following would turn you purple?

1. Your boss fires you for no reason.
2. The police arrest you by mistake.
3. Your car breaks down and you get to work late.
4. Someone steals your car.

THE FACTS OF LIFE
Home Remedies

In chapter 2, you looked up the telephone numbers of the police station and fire station in your neighborhood.

In this chapter, a young woman swallowed too much aspirin. It may seem strange, but the most dangerous items in your house are the things we usually think are safe, for example, aspirin. This year about 500,000 children in America will accidentally poison themselves.

In the past, when a child swallowed poison, you were told to make the child vomit. Things are no longer that simple. New and different chemical poisons require different treatment. If your child swallows poison, it is a good idea to call *Poison Control* or your doctor immediately. If you go to the hospital, be sure to take the bottle of medicine (or chemicals) with you.

What about those small accidents that happen every day: the stove burns, the knife cuts, and the scraped knees? You can't always run to the doctor.

The first thing to do is decide if the injury is serious—serious enough to go to the hospital. If it is, go right

Aloe

away. Don't wait until morning or wait for a few hours to see how you feel. If the injury is serious, go to the hospital immediately.

If you decide it isn't serious, there are many home remedies you can use. To treat small burns, for example, many people keep an aloe plant in the house. When they burn themselves, they rub the juice of the aloe leaf on the burn. The easiest thing to do is to run cold water on the burn.

To heal cuts and scrapes, there are many things you can buy in the drugstore, such as antibiotic creams. But if you get a serious cut or are cut by something rusty, you should probably go to a doctor and get a tetanus shot (injection).

Remember, when you are calling a doctor or the hospital, keep calm and keep speaking English.

EXERCISES

1. Bring a bottle or a can from home. Bring one that has a "Warning" label on it. This label will tell you what to do in case of an accident. Read the label in class and discuss the vocabulary. (Look for cans or bottles of drain opener, aspirin, petroleum jelly, nail polish remover, decongestants, etc.)
2. A child just swallowed a whole bottle of vitamins. Get together with another student—one of you will report the emergency. The other will be the doctor or the person at the poison control center who receives the call.
3. Describe home remedies you know to treat burns, cuts, and scrapes. Are there some you wouldn't use?
4. Describe an accident that happened to you, or someone in your family, at home. How did you treat it?

See supplementary exercises on page 156.

RTEENTHIRTEEN

Some questions you might like to discuss with your classmates:

Do you remember any of the people you went to school with when you were younger?

Are you still friends with them?

What has happened to them? Are they successful? Did any of them have problems?

Say these words

after your teacher or after an American friend. You'll find these words in the story.

a·head'
com·plain'
foot'·ball
grad·u·a'·tion
jun'·ior
once
per'·jur·y
re'·cog·nize
sex'·y
shake
steal
team
trust

slang
big boys
fin'·ish (*someone*) off
girl scout
junk'·ie
nick'·el and dime
push'·er

phrases
be set for life
be set
drop out (v.)
hide out (v.)
show up

In this chapter we learn more about Henry di Bernardo and who his friends were.

As you read, think about these questions:

Did anyone on 88th Street know Henry?
Did Willie lie to the police?
What happened to Henry in his junior year in high school?
What did Henry want from Clara?
Why was Henry on the roof of 229 88th Street?

YOU CAN FOOL SOME OF THE PEOPLE SOME OF THE TIME

(Amanda Fielding and Clara Torres are sitting on the front steps.)

Amanda: Shh. Here he comes. Isn't he gorgeous?
Clara: I guess so.
Amanda: He's so sexy I could die.
Willie: Hi, girls.
Amanda: Hi, Willie.
Clara: Hi.
Willie: What's happening? What are you two doing out here?
Clara: Talking. How are *you* doing?
Willie: Can't complain.
Clara: That's not what I hear.
Willie: *(looking at Amanda)* And I thought I could trust your father. The whole neighborhood probably knows by now.
Amanda: I don't know what you mean.
Willie: Last night . . . with your father.
Amanda: What are you talking about?
Willie: So you don't know. Okay. *(looking at Clara)* So what *did* you mean?
Clara: The thing with Bernie.
Willie: Bernie. Bernie who?
Clara: Henry di Bernardo. The guy you found on the roof.
Willie: Oh, him. I never called him "Bernie."
Clara: Aha! So you *did* know him! I thought so.
Willie: Hey, listen. I hardly knew him at all. How'd *you* know him?
Clara: From school. He was on the football team his junior year. All the girls were crazy about him.
Amanda: So what happened?
Clara: I don't know. Something went wrong. His grades went down. He got sick and couldn't play anymore. He just seemed to lose interest in everything.
Amanda: Too bad.
Clara: Yeah. He dropped out of school two months before graduation.
Amanda: Why? Do you know?
Clara: He told me that he was all set to make a lot of money, and he was going to be set for life.

Willie: Some life—it didn't last very long.

Amanda: Was he in with somebody big?

Willie: That's what he liked to think. But he was just a nickel and dime pusher at the disco. I bought some stuff from him once or twice.

Clara: So why did you tell the police you didn't know him?

Willie: I didn't recognize him at first. And then, when I got a good look at him and saw who he was, I said to myself, "Hey, Willie, forget him. He's dead."

Amanda: You lied? To the police?

Willie: Are you a girl scout, or something? Why should I tell the police that I knew a junkie?

Clara: He wasn't a junkie.

Willie: Sure he was. Why do you think he started pushing? He had to get money somehow.

Clara: You're wrong. Bernie was a nice guy. He may have sold some stuff now and then, but he was going to get out of that.

Willie: Hey, how well *did* you know him?

Clara: Well enough.

Amanda: Really? Did you parents know?

Clara: Of course not. Papa wouldn't have let him in the front door.

Willie:	Wait a minute. Don't tell me. Let me guess. You used to meet him on the roof, right?
Clara:	So what if I did? I hadn't seen him for about a month. He said he had some business somewhere else for a while.
Willie:	I'll bet. He was probably hiding out. He probably stole from the big boys and they finished him off.
Clara:	No. I . . . No.
Amanda:	Clara, I'm so sorry. You really liked him, didn't you?
Clara:	He was so . . . .
Amanda:	I think he liked you a lot. He was probably trying to see you at the end.
Clara:	He called and asked if I had any money. I was going to give him everything I made last summer. But he never showed up.
Amanda:	Oh.
Willie:	You're lucky. You saved yourself some money.
Amanda:	(to Willie) Hey, listen you. You think you're so smart. What are you going to do when the police find out you lied? Ever heard of perjury?
Willie:	Sure, but who's going to tell them?
Clara:	They'll find out.
Willie:	Don't worry.
Amanda:	Who's worrying?

(Willie goes into the building. Clara is staring at the step and shaking her head slowly. Amanda reaches over puts her hand on Clara's arm.)

Amanda:	Don't worry, I'll never say anything to anyone. Willie won't, either, I'm sure.
Clara:	I can't believe he just wanted my money.
Amanda:	Maybe he didn't.
Clara:	You're nice, Amanda.
Amanda:	Mmmm. But, listen here, girl! Don't ever let me catch you being so dumb again, hear?
Clara:	Uh huh.

CULTURAL NOTES

1. Americans love sports. In high school, most young men play some kind of sport like basketball, football, baseball, or hockey. Good players are usually very popular in school. There's a song that begins, "You gotta (have to) be a football hero to get along with a beautiful girl."
   - *Who are the "heroes" or most popular students in your country?*
2. The Girl Scouts and the Boy Scouts are international organizations. They teach young boys and girls about nature and how to take care of themselves. They also teach children to be honest and good.
3. High school and college students often take jobs in the summer to earn extra money. They usually work in supermarkets, in stores, in restaurants, and in summer resorts. Because there are more students than jobs, summer jobs are hard to find and are often low-paying.
   - *Have you ever had a summer job? Would you ever work as a streetcleaner or a dishwasher?*

COMPREHENSION EXERCISES
Face the Facts

If the sentence is true, write "T." If the sentence is false, write "F."

1. ___ Willie knew Bernie very well.

2. ___ Willie lied to the police when he made his statement.

3. ___ Bernie used to meet Clara on the roof.

4. ___ Bernie never finished high school.

5. ___ Clara thought Bernie was a nice guy.

Read Between the Lines

If the sentence is true, write "T." If the sentence is false, write "F." Make an inference.

1. ___ Amanda thinks Willie is more attractive than Clara does.

2. ___ George Fielding, Amanda's father, told everyone about his conversation with Willie.

3. ___ Henry di Bernardo was a junkie.

4. ___ Bernie probably became a junkie in high school.

5. ___ Amanda is a girl scout.

MORE DIFFICULT COMPREHENSION EXERCISES
Find the Supporting Details

1. Willie says that Bernie was a junkie. Find some information in this story or previous ones that supports what he said.

2. Willie now believes that Bernie was killed. What does he think happened?

Make a Judgment

Did Bernie care for Clara, or didn't he? Discuss your opinion and your reasons for it with your classmates.

VOCABULARY EXERCISES

Mind Your Words

be set
drop out
hide out

Look at the following exercises. They will help you understand how these phrases are used. You may use your dictionary to find their definitions. Remember, we are working with the meanings of the phrases as they appear in the dialogue: they may have other meanings in other contexts.

BE SET
"He was all set to make a lot of money."

The best synonym for *set* as used in the example above is:
1. able
2. ready
3. happy
4. willing

In the sense that *was all set* is used in the example, it also means that di Bernardo:
1. was prepared to make a lot of money

2. didn't know how to make a lot of money
3. had no connections who could help him make a lot of money

DROP OUT
"He dropped out of school."

Another way to say, *"He dropped out of school,"* is:
1. He failed.
2. The teachers made him leave school.
3. He left or quit school before graduating.

When somebody *drops out of* something, they leave:
1. voluntarily (because they want to)
2. because they have to

Which of the following institutions or organizations can a person drop out of without much trouble?
1. the army
2. school, when you are thirteen years old
3. a social club
4. jail
5. school, when you are seventeen years old
6. college

HIDE OUT
"He was probably hiding out."
Find the sentence above in the story. How long do you

think di Bernardo was hiding out?

1. an hour
2. a day
3. a week
4. a month or more

When somebody *hides out*, it means two things:

1. somebody or some people are looking for him
2. he probably did something illegal or wrong

Do you think di Bernardo was hiding out for the reasons stated above in (1.) and (2.)? _____

Which of the following people might hide out?

1. killers
2. thieves
3. secretaries
4. housewives
5. children

THE FACTS OF LIFE

More About American Schools

Elementary and high schools begin each year in September and end in June. In most states, students must go to school until they are sixteen years old. Students usually have the summer months free. The school week begins on Monday and students go every day until Friday. The school day usually begins between 8:00 and 8:30 a.m. and ends each afternoon between 2:30 and 3:00. Kindergarten usually ends at noon.

In elementary schools, most children have one teacher and stay in the same room all day. In middle school and high school, the students have different teachers and move from class to class.

At the college level, the school year usually begins in September and ends in May or June. Some students go to school in the summer to take classes they want or need. The school year is often divided into *semesters*—one in the fall, one in the spring. Each semester is usually fifteen weeks long.

In college, students get *credits* for classes. If students spend three hours a week in class for one course, they will get three credits if they pass the course at the end of the semester. Most students take about five courses (fifteen credits) each semester. Most American colleges grant a B.A. or a B.S. when the student has earned between 120 and 130 credits.

The following is the grading system used by many schools in the U.S.:

Excellent	....	(A)	90-100%
Very Good	....	(B)	80-89%
Average	....	(C)	70-79%
Poor	....	(D)	60-69%
Failing	....	(F)	0-59%

When a high school or college has four different levels (years), they have the following names:

The Year	Name for the Year	Name for Student
first year	freshman year	a freshman
second year	sophomore year	a sophomore
third year	junior year	a junior
fourth year	senior year	a senior

About fifty percent of American high school graduates go to some kind of college. Of these, only about half finally graduate. These figures are important because in most European countries and Latin American countries, only about five percent of the student population ever gets the opportunity to go to a university.

EXERCISES

1. In small groups, choose several of the following questions about *your country* and discuss them.
   1. How many years must children go to school in your country?
   2. During what months do children go to school?
   3. How many hours a day do children study?
   4. Are there any holidays from school during the year?
2. In small groups, choose several of the following questions and discuss them.
   1. How many years should children be required to go to school?
   2. Should teachers give grades or should they only say if a student passes or fails?
   3. Should students go to school all year or should they have a two-month vacation?

FOURTEEN

Some questions you might like to discuss with your classmates:

Have you ever seen the police arrest anyone in real life or on television? What do the police do?

Say these words

after your teacher or after an American friend.

ap·point'
ar·rest' (v.)
be·hind'
court
cri'·mi·nal
hand'·cuff
jail
law'·yer
Ma'am

mis·un·der·stand'·ing
pre'·sent
reach (v.)
right (n.)
spread
sta'·tion
war'·rant
wea'·pon
wish

phrases
be not all there
be used a·gainst'
   (someone)
face the mu'·sic
mixed up
out of *(someone's)*
   hands
o'·ver my dead
   bod'·y
un'·der ar·rest'

In this chapter Willie gets into deeper trouble with the police.

As you read, think about the following questions:

Why do the police go to Willie's apartment?
What did Willie do wrong?
What does Sally want to do?
Where do the police take Willie?
Why does Mrs. Gold try to stop them?

FACING THE MUSIC

(There is a knock at the door. Willie gets up and goes to answer it.)

Willie: Who is it? Sally?
Police: The police. Open up.

(Willie opens the door.)

Police: Are you William Dorio?
Willie: Yes. What is this?
Police: Can we come in?
Willie: Why?
Police: Do you want to discuss this in the hall?
Willie: What do you want?
Police: All right, Mr. Dorio. We have a warrant for your arrest. You have the right to remain silent. Anything you say can and will be used against you in a court of law. You have the right to speak with a lawyer before we question you and to have your lawyer with you during questioning. If you cannot afford a lawyer, one will be appointed for you before questioning if you wish one. If you decide to answer questions now, without a lawyer present, you have the right to stop answering at any time. Do you understand what I've just said?

Willie: Yes. What are you arresting me for?
Police: Perjury. Turn around. Hands on the wall. Spread your legs.
(The policeman checks to see if Willie has any weapons on him.)
Okay. Turn around. Put your hands behind you.
(The policeman puts handcuffs on Willie.)

Willie: Hey, are these necessary?
Police: Okay. Let's go.
Willie: Where are we going?
Police: To the station. Let's go.
Willie: Wait a second. Do you have to take me in?
Police: Let's go.

(They start down the stairs. As they reach the fourth floor, the door of 4W opens. Emily looks out. She sees Willie and the two policemen.)

Emily: What's happening? Willie, what is it?
Willie: Tell Sally I can't see her tonight.

Emily:	What?
	(She sees the handcuffs on Willie.)
	What's happened?
Willie:	Just a misunderstanding.
	(from inside the apartment)
Sally:	Emily, what's happening?
Emily:	Nothing.
Sally:	*(walking to the door)* What is it? Something's going on. *(She sees Willie in handcuffs.)* Willie!

Police:	Let's go. Keep moving.
Sally:	Wait a minute. He's a friend of mine.
	(to Willie) Willie, what's going on?

(Clara Torres looks out her door.)

Willie:	They're arresting me.
Sally:	Why?
Willie:	Perjury, they say.
Clara:	Hey, Papa. They're arresting Willie!

(Willie and the police continue down the stairs. Sally, Emily, and Clara watch. Then Sally goes back into her apartment and comes out with her coat.)

Emily: Where do you think you're going?

Sally: I'm going after them.

Emily: Over my dead body. You're not going anywhere. I told you not to get mixed up with him. I told you he was trouble.

Sally: Oh, Emily, for God's sake. He's my friend.

Emily: Sally, please, please don't get mixed up in this. Please. Think about it until morning. Please, Sally.

(Willie and the police reach the first floor. Mrs. Gold is standing in the hall in front of the door.)

Mrs. Gold: Now, what's this all about?

Police: Please step out of the way, ma'am.

Mrs. Gold: Not until I find out what's going on here.

Police: I don't want to have to move you, Ma'am . . . or arrest you.

Mrs. Gold: You'd do that to an eighty-year old lady? What's this world coming to?

Willie: It's all right, Mrs. Gold.

Mrs. Gold: Just someone tell me what's going on. That's all I ask.

Police: He's under arrest.

Mrs. Gold: Now, Officers, I know this young man. He's a fine young man.

Police: Listen, lady . . . .

Mrs. Gold: Mrs. Gold. Rebecca Gold. Some people call me Rebecca, but I prefer Becky, myself.

Police: Let us by. We have a warrant for his arrest. It's out of our hands. We're just doing our job.

Mrs. Gold: There must be some mistake. Can't we talk this over? Come in. Have some coffee.

Police: No ma'am. Step aside.

Willie: It's okay, Mrs. Gold.

Mrs. Gold: Well, if you're going to jail, I'm going, too.

Willie: *(to the police)* She's a little old—not all there—if you know what I mean.

Mrs. Gold: Old? There's nothing wrong with me. And if you think I'm just going to let you take him away and put him with all those criminals . . . well, you're wrong.

(George Fielding comes down the stairs.)

George: What's going on here?

Mrs. Gold: They're arresting Willie and me.

Police: Look, lady . . . .

Mrs. Gold: Mrs. Gold to you.

Police: . . . move out of the way.

Willie: Please, Mrs. Gold. Do as they say. Mr. Fielding? Make her move.

George: Mrs. Gold, it's all right. Let's stand over here. Come on.

Mrs. Gold: No. I'm not going to stand over there.

George: It's all right. We'll follow them down to the station. I'll go with you. Okay?

Mrs. Gold: Well, all right. I'll just get my things. Don't you worry, Willie. We'll be right behind you. This is a free country. They just can't go around arresting innocent people.

Police: Let's go.

(They walk out the front door.)

Mrs. Gold: I won't be a minute, George. They haven't heard the last of Becky Gold.

CULTURAL NOTES

1. When we do not know the name of an older woman, we often call her *ma'am*. Men often use this more than women:

   "Excuse me *ma'am*, is this your glove?"

   With younger women and with women who work in stores and restaurants, we often use *miss:*

   "*Miss*, may I have a glass of water?"

   However, when you know or are expected to know the woman's name, you must use her name:

   "*Mrs. Gold,* how are you feeling today?"

2. Mrs. Gold is around eighty years old. Because of her age, the police treat Mrs. Gold more tolerantly than they would if she were younger.

   • *Are older people treated with respect in your country?*

COMPREHENSION EXERCISES
Face the Facts

If the sentence is true, write "T." If the sentence is false, write "F."

1. ___ The police arrest Willie for murder.

2. ___ Willie asks to have a lawyer.

3. ___ Mrs. Gold wants to know why the police are taking Willie away.

4. ___ Willie tells the police that Mrs. Gold is a little crazy.

5. ___ George promises to take Mrs. Gold to the station.

Read Between the Lines

If the sentence is true, write "T." If the sentence is false, write "F." Make an inference.

1. ___ The police find a weapon on Willie.

2. ___ Willie doesn't want to tell Emily why he's been arrested.

3. ___ Sally doesn't want to do anything to help Willie.

4. ___ The policemen don't have to arrest Willie if they don't want to.

5. ___ Willie doesn't want Mrs. Gold to get into trouble with the police.

MORE DIFFICULT COMPREHENSION EXERCISES
Find the Supporting Details

In the story, the police "read Willie his rights."

This means that the police tell Willie what he can do and what he doesn't have to do when he is arrested. The police tell him he has three rights. What are they?

1. _____

2. _____

3. _____

Make a Judgment

Do you think that there is anything that Willie could have done to make the police treat him with more sympathy?

VOCABULARY EXERCISES
Mind Your Words

mixed up with, involved with (from chapter 9)
not all there

Look at the following exercises. They will help you understand how these phrases are used. You may use your dictionary to find their definitions. Remember, we are working with the meanings of the phrases as they appear in the dialogue; they may have other meanings in other contexts.

MIXED UP WITH, INVOLVED WITH

Example 1: "I told you not to get *mixed up with* him."
Example 2: "*He's involved with* the boy who got murdered on the roof."

Look at the following six examples:

1. correct: He was *mixed up with* some bad characters.
2. correct: He was *involved with* some bad characters.
3. incorrect: He was *mixed up with* Einstein on an important scientific project.
4. correct: He was *involved with* Einstein on an important scientific project.
5. incorrect: He is *mixed up with* a wonderful girl.
6. correct: He is *involved* with a wonderful girl.

After studying the examples above, decide whether the following statements are true or false.

1. ___ *Mixed up with* has a negative connotation.

2. ___ *Involved with* has a positive connotation only.

3. ___ *Mixed up with* and *involved with* have similar meaning.

4. ___ *Involved with* can be used more widely than *mixed up with*.

5. ___ *Involved with* can have romantic connotations.

NOT ALL THERE

"She's a little old—*not all there*—if you know what I mean."

Not all there is a slang expression that means that the person's mind is not working very well.

From this we can probably say that the phrase *not all there* is:

1. scientific
2. medical
3. unscientific

THE FACTS OF LIFE
An Arrest

In this chapter Willie was arrested. The American system of law is similar to the law in some countries and different from the law in others.

Generally speaking, when a person is arrested in the U.S., the following is true:

1. The police must tell you that they are the police before they arrest you or touch you.
2. The police cannot enter your home without your permission or without a search warrant.

5. At the time of arrest, the police must explain what legal rights you have.
6. In the U.S., our system of law assumes that a person is innocent until proven guilty. Therefore, if you do not want to answer questions or give information, you do not have to. The police or the D.A. has to get the evidence to prove you are guilty.
7. If you have money and if you want a lawyer, you can pay for one to be with you when you speak to the police. If you do not have any money or if you do not know a lawyer, you can ask the police or the court to give you a lawyer. The state will pay the lawyer to watch out for your rights.

There is an old saying: A man who defends himself has a fool for a lawyer. In other words, you should always get a lawyer to help you rather than defend yourself.

EXERCISES

1. Compare the system of law in your country to the legal system in the United States.
2. Find an article in the newspaper that describes an arrest in the U.S. or another country. Discuss the article in class.
3. Watch a police program on TV. What do the police do when they arrest someone? Write down what you see.

See supplementary exercises on page 156.

3. The police must show a judge that they have good reason to believe that something illegal is going on in your home before the judge will give the police a search warrant.
4. The police must tell you why you have been arrested soon after the arrest or else the police must let you go free.

FIFTEEN

FIFTEEN

Some questions you might like to discuss with your classmates:

Have you ever been to a police station in the U.S.?
What did you see there?
Have you ever needed a lawyer? What for?

Say these words
after your teacher or after an American friend.

ac·cuse'
brown'·ie
cook'·ie
con'·tents (n.)
co·op'·er·ate
eas'·i·ly
faint
ice cream
is'·sue (v.)
judge (n.)
kill
mark (v.)
nut (food)
o·ver·come'

par'·lor
pa·trol'·man
pho'·to·graph
pos'·si·ble
rub'·bish
scar
threat

phrases
choc'·o·late chip
file fold'·er
a full moon
get rid of
hold back

pay the pip'·er
play dumb
run a·long'
think *(something)*
  o'·ver
We shall o·ver·come'.
We shall not be
  moved.

slang
dope
finish off
get *(someone)* cold
the mob (n.)

nut (person)
pop'·py·cock
punk
wise

*legal words/police
  terms*
book (v.)
charge (v. & n.)
cell
fin'·ger·print (v. & n.)
sus·pi'·cion

*legal phrases/police
  phrases*
a for'·mal charge
lock *(someone)* up
ob·struct'·ing just'·ice
ser'·geant
throw the book at
  (someone)

In this chapter, Willie is taken to the police station and questioned.

As you read think about these questions:

Why does Mrs. Gold want to stay at the police station?

How serious is the crime of perjury?

How long might Willie have to spend in jail?

What do the police want to know when they question him?

Who does Willie seem to care most about at the end of the story?

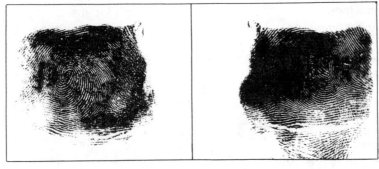

PAYING THE PIPER

(At the 92nd Street police station, the two patrolmen walk in with Willie.)

Desk Sergeant:	Well, what do we have here?
Police:	Suspicion of perjury. A warrant issued.
Desk Sergeant:	Okay. Name?
Police:	Tell him your name.
Willie:	What? Oh, sure. William Dorio.
Desk Sergeant:	D-O-R-I-O?
Willie:	Yes.
Desk Sergeant:	Address?

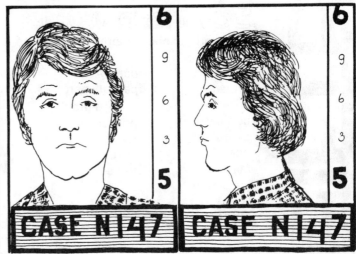

Willie:	229 88th Street.
Desk Sergeant:	You're being booked for the crime of perjury.
Willie:	Crime?
Desk Sergeant:	Do you understand?
Willie:	Yes.
Desk Sergeant:	*(to the patrolmen)* Have you read him his rights?
Police:	Yes.
Desk Sergeant:	Do you understand your rights?
Willie:	Yes.
Desk Sergeant:	Okay, take him down and fingerprint and photograph him.

(Mrs. Gold and George Fielding arrive at the station a minute after Willie has been taken downstairs.)

Mrs. Gold:	Where is he?
Desk Sergeant:	Can I help you?
Mrs. Gold:	Willie Dorio. What have you done with him?
Desk Sergeant:	Who are you?
Mrs. Gold:	Mrs. Rebecca Gold. And who are you, young man?
Desk Sergeant:	Sergeant Murphy.
Mrs. Gold:	Well, Sergeant Murphy, where's Willie?
Sergeant Murphy:	Are you a relative?
Mrs. Gold:	I'm his friend and I'm here to make sure you treat him right, the poor boy.
Sergeant Murphy:	*(to George)* And you?
George:	George Fielding. A friend of Mrs. Gold and Willie. What's the charge, Sergeant?
Sergeant Murphy:	Well, Mr. Fielding, he's been charged with perjury.
George:	How serious is that?
Sergeant Murphy:	All crimes are serious.
George:	*How* serious?
Sergeant Murphy:	Let me see. *(looking in a book on his desk)* Perjury . . . one to five.
Mrs. Gold:	What did you say?
Sergeant Murphy:	Perjury. One to five years.
Mrs. Gold:	Five years? Oh, oh . . . oh . . . my heart!
George:	She's going to faint! Get a chair!

(George holds Mrs. Gold while Sergeant Murphy brings a chair. They sit her down.)

Sergeant Murphy:	I'll call an ambulance.
Mrs. Gold:	Oh . . . mmmm . . . that's better.
George:	Mrs. Gold, are you all right? How do you feel?
Mrs. Gold:	Willie. Poor Willie. My poor boy.
George:	Mrs. Gold!
Mrs. Gold:	Hmmm?

George:	How do you feel?
Mrs. Gold:	Me? Feel?

(Mrs. Gold sits up in the chair. Sergeant Murphy is talking on the police radio.)

Sergeant Murphy:	. . . send an ambulance.
Mrs. Gold:	Ambulance? Who's sick?
George:	You are.

Mrs. Gold:	Poppycock. I'm fine. *(shaking her finger at Sergeant Murphy)* Do you think you can get rid of me that easily? I'm not moving.
Sergeant Murphy:	*(on the radio)* Forget the ambulance. *(to Mrs. Gold)* Suit yourself, ma'am, but you've got a long wait ahead.
Mrs. Gold:	That's all right. I brought some cake and cookies along with me right here in

	my bag. We shall overcome, Sergeant, and we shall not be moved.
George:	How long will it be?
Sergeant Murphy:	He has to be questioned and then it takes around seventy-two hours before he goes before a judge for formal charges.
George:	That's three days! Mrs. Gold . . . .
Mrs. Gold:	We shall overcome. Sergeant, would you like a cookie?
Sergeant Murphy:	There must be a full moon. I always get the nuts.
Mrs. Gold:	Nuts? No. I make my chocolate chip cookies without nuts. My brownies have nuts. Would you like a brownie? I brought some of them, too.

(Willie and a policeman come back into the room.)

Mrs. Gold:	Willie!
Willie:	Mrs. Gold! Mr. Fielding! What are you doing here?
Mrs. Gold:	You don't think I would let you come here all alone, do you? Would you like a cookie?
Policeman:	Don't give him anything.
Mrs. Gold:	It's just a cookie.
Policeman:	Nothing. Let's go. In here.

(The policeman unlocks a door, puts Willie in the room, comes back out and locks the door.)

Policeman:	*(to the Sergeant)* Okay. He's ready for questioning.
George:	*(to Mrs. Gold)* Mrs. Gold, we're not doing any good here. Let's go home.
Mrs. Gold:	You run along, George. I'm going to stay.
George:	I can't leave you here.
Mrs. Gold:	Of course you can. Sergeant Murphy will take care of me, won't you, Sergeant? You run along.
George:	Are you sure?
Mrs. Gold:	Of course! Now, Sergeant, tell me about your family . . . .

(An hour later two detectves enter the room where Willie is sitting alone. They are reading the contents of a file folder marked, "William Dorio.")

Detective Moses:	I'm Detective Moses and this is Detective Donlevy. William Dorio?
Willie:	Yes.
Detective Moses:	You're in a lot of trouble, kid.
Willie:	What do you mean?
Detective Moses:	Don't play dumb with us.
Willie:	Hey, look. I'm not . . . .

Detective Moses:	You can spend five years in jail if we throw the book at you.
Willie:	What do you want out of me?
Detective Donlevy:	Why don't you cooperate with us and we'll see what we can do for you?
Willie:	I don't have to say anything.
Detective Moses:	That's right. Come on. We're wasting our time. Lock him up.

(Detective Moses stands up and goes to the door.)

Detective Donlevy:	Just answer a few questions.
Willie:	What kind of questions?
Detective Donlevy:	Do you want a lawyer?
Willie:	What kind of questions?
Detective Donlevy:	You found the body, right?
Willie:	I guess so.
Detective Donlevy:	"I guess so," what does that mean?
Willie:	I reported finding the body, yes.
Detective Moses:	Cute. He's a real cute one.
Detective Donlevy:	Did you kill him, son?
Willie:	No!
Detective Moses:	What, then? Did you get into a fight? He threatened you and you finished him off?
Willie:	No!
Detective Donlevy:	Why did you lie, son?
Willie:	When did I lie?
Detective Moses:	Listen. You made a signed statement.

	And we've got you cold.
Detective Donlevy:	Why did you do it?
Willie:	I've got nothing to say.
Detective Moses:	All right, listen. We've got you on perjury and we can even get you on obstructing justice. Think it over, kid. It's your life.

(They get up and go out. Willie is alone again in the room. A half hour later Detective Moses goes back in the room.)

Detective Moses:	Well, have you thought it over?
Willie:	Yeah. I still don't know where I lied.
Detective Moses:	Did you kill diBernardo?
Willie:	No.
Detective Moses:	Did you know diBernardo?
Willie:	When?
Detective Moses:	When? You're sitting here accused of perjury and you're asking *me* questions?
Willie:	Okay. Maybe I've seen him once or twice.
Detective Moses:	Oh? Where?
Willie:	Around.
Detective Moses:	Around where?
Willie:	Around 86th Street, the disco.
Detective Moses:	All right, now we're getting somewhere. So you knew him.
Willie:	I didn't say that. I said I'd seen him around.

Detective Moses:	What was he doing when you saw him around?
Willie:	What do you mean?
Detective Moses:	You know what I mean. You bought

	dope from him, didn't you?
Willie:	No.
Detective Moses:	You're really asking for it. You want to have me throw another count of perjury at you? Five more years, Dorio?
Willie:	Listen. I saw him around. Everyone knew who he was. But I didn't know him well or anything. I didn't even know his name.
Detective Moses:	Did you ever buy any stuff from him?
Willie:	I'm not going to answer that.

(Detective Donlevy comes in the room.)

Detective Donlevy:	Take a break. There's an old lady outside giving out cookies and getting Murphy's life story.
Willie:	Mrs. Gold.
Detective Donlevy:	You know her? Bet you're glad you're in here.
Willie:	She's a nice old lady.

(Detective Donlevy and Detective Moses go to a corner of the room and speak softly for a minute. Detective Moses leaves the room.)

| Detective Donlevy: | Okay, William. So you knew diBernardo and you knew he was a pusher. Why didn't you tell us that in the first place? |

Willie:	I didn't want to get involved.
Detective Donlevy:	So why'd you report the body?
Willie:	I didn't realize who it was.
Detective Donlevy:	Okay. Let's say I believe you. You're in a lot of trouble here for making a false statement. If I were you, I'd cooperate.
Willie:	What do you want from me?
Detective Donlevy:	Why do you think he was killed?
Willie:	He probably held back money or stuff from the mob.
Detective Donlevy:	Why do you think he did that?
Willie:	He was a junkie.
Detective Donlevy:	Who did he work for?
Willie:	How do I know?
Detective Donlevy:	Did you ever see him with anyone else? Did he have any friends?
Willie:	I don't know. I told you I hardly knew him.
Detective Donlevy:	I'll show you some pictures. See if you recognize any of them.
Willie:	What will it do for me?
Detective Donlevy:	We'll see.

(Detective Donlevy goes out and comes back with some pictures. He puts them on the table in front of Willie. Detective Moses enters.)

Detective Donlevy:	I want you to take a good look at these. Did you ever see any of them with diBernardo?
Willie:	*(looking at the pictures)* I never saw this old guy. And . . . .
Detective Moses:	Look hard, kid.
Willie:	Uh . . . this young guy with the scar . . . he looks . . . .
Detective Donlevy:	Did you ever see him with diBernardo?
Willie:	Maybe. I'm not sure.
Detective Moses:	"Maybe." What's this "maybe"? Did you or didn't you?
Willie:	I told you I'm not sure.
Detective Donlevy:	What about the others?
Willie:	I don't know. I'm tired.
Detective Moses:	Did you or didn't you?
Willie:	How can I be sure? The disco's dark and there are crazy lights all over the place. El Alto isn't exactly an ice cream parlor, you know.
Detective Moses:	Don't get cute with me, punk. I asked you a question.
Willie:	I want a lawyer.
Detective Donlevy:	Okay, okay son. You're going to jail. You can see a lawyer in the morning.
Willie:	I have to spend the night in jail?
Detective Moses:	What did you expect? Let's go.

(They lead Willie out to the cellblock. As they pass the main

desk, they see Mrs. Gold.)

Mrs. Gold:	Willie! Are they letting you go?
Willie:	Nothing to worry about. I'll be out of here tomorrow morning.
Mrs. Gold:	Why not right now? We can go home together.
Willie:	Uh . . . I have to see a judge first, but why don't you go home? I'm okay now.
Mrs. Gold:	Well, maybe . . . all right, if you say so.
Willie:	Will you do me a favor?
Mrs. Gold:	Certainly.
Willie:	Do you know a lawyer?
Mrs. Gold:	I'm sure I do.
Willie:	Will you call him, and ask him to help me?
Mrs. Gold:	Of course.
Willie:	And Mrs. Gold?
Mrs. Gold:	Yes?
Willie:	Will you tell Sally I'm all right. And . . . call this number *(Willie gives Mrs. Gold a piece of paper.)* and tell my parents what happened. No. Forget it. *(He takes the paper back.)* Just tell Sally I'm all right. And, Mrs. Gold . . . .
Mrs. Gold:	Yes, Willie dear?
Willie:	Thanks. I'll see you in the morning.

CULTURAL NOTES

1. *We Shall Overcome* is the anthem of the civil rights movement. It was frequently heard at demonstrations in the 1960s where blacks were demanding civil, social, and economic equality. It was also heard in the 1970s when people were protesting against war and nuclear power. For many Americans, that song means that they will be patient and peaceful, but they will not give up.

The first part of the song is:

We shall overcome
We shall overcome
We shall overcome someday.
Deep in my heart
I do believe
We shall overcome someday.

- *How do people in your country protest? Is there a famous protest song?*

COMPREHENSION EXERCISES
Face the Facts

If the sentence is true, write "T." If the sentence is false, write "F."

1. ___ Willie is booked for killing Henry diBernardo.

2. ___ People who commit perjury have to spend as many as five years in jail.

3. ___ Mrs. Gold almost faints.

4. ___ Willie identifies two men he saw with diBernardo.

5. ___ Willie wants Mrs. Gold to call Sally.

Read Between the Lines

If the sentence is true, write "T." If the sentence is false, write "F." Make an inference.

1. ___ Willie tells the police all he knows about Henry diBernardo.

2. ___ Mrs. Gold likes Willie very much.

3. ___ Mrs. Gold stays at the station because she is afraid that the police will hurt Willie.

4. ___ Mrs. Gold stays at the station because she wants Willie to know she cares about him.

5. ___ The police broke the law when they made Willie answer questions without his lawyer.

MORE DIFFICULT COMPREHENSION EXERCISES

Find the Supporting Details

When someone is taken to the police station because there is a warrant for his arrest, five things happen to him at the station. Look at the story and see if you can find the first four.

1.

2.

3.

4.

5. The person is locked up.

Make a Judgment

1. Do you think that Willie should have spoken to the police without a lawyer present? Discuss your opinion and your reasons for it with your classmates.
2. Do you think Willie will have to spend a year or more in jail? Discuss your opinion with your classmates.
3. Do you think Willie's crime (perjury) is serious, and deserves one to five years?

VOCABULARY EXERCISES

Mind Your Words

nut

full moon

Look at the following exercises. They will help you understand how these items are used. You may use your dictionary to find their definitions. Remember, we are working with the meanings of the items as they appear in the dialogue; they may have other meanings in other contexts.

NUT
Example 1: "I always get the *nuts.*"
Example 2: "My brownies have *nuts.*"

Find the example in the story. When Sgt. Murphy says *nuts*, he means:
1. peanuts
2. the moon
3. cookies
4. strange or crazy people

We imagine that Mrs. Gold doesn't hear the Sergeant clearly. If Mrs. Gold knew that the Sergeant thought she was a nut, she would probably be:
1. offended
2. very angry
3. pleased

As with many other words in English, when you call a person a *nut*, you can be critical or you can use it as an

affectionate term. In the situations below, are the speakers being critical or affectionate?
1. Henry, I love to watch you dance. You're such a nut.
2. I'll never work with that guy again. He's a nut, a real nut.
3. I don't care what you say. A man who was responsible for so many people's dying had to be a nut.
4. She's really a nut. You never know what she's going to do next. Last week she decided she wanted to walk from New York to San Francisco.

FULL MOON

"There must be a *full moon*."

Many people believe that the moon affects human behavior. There is no "scientific proof" of this, but many people believe it anyway. A friend told us that some hospitals schedule extra doctors and nurses for the emergency room on the night of a full moon. These hospitals have found that people have more accidents at

that time. What is not an accident is that the English word *lunatic* comes from the Latin word *luna,* meaning *moon.*

Nowadays people use this expression figuratively. People will say, *There must be a full moon,* to indicate the presence of a *nut*—whether or not the moon is really full.

Sergeant Murphy may believe that the moon has something to do with:
1. the number of cookies he gets
2. the number of crazy people he sees
3. the number of arrests that are made

Sergeant Murphy is probably:
1. used to dealing with nuts
2. afraid of nuts
3. amused by nuts

When he says, *"There must be a full moon,"* it probably means:
1. He thinks Mrs. Gold is dangerous.
2. She is so crazy he will need help to control her.
3. He thinks Mrs. Gold is criminally insane.
4. He will have to treat her differently from the ordinary people who come in.

THE FACTS OF LIFE

Why People Choose Cities!

Very often the facts of life, as we have presented them in these pages, have been unpleasant or, at best, serious. But there is a bright side to urban American life.

For every person who hates the city, you can find one who wouldn't live anywhere else. Whatever your

interests are, you can always find people to share them in the city.

People like to say that life in large urban areas like New York or Chicago or Los Angeles is lonely and largely unhappy. But this is not necessarily true. A big city, even New York, is not really just one city. It is a collection of dozens or perhaps hundreds of neighborhoods, small villages, within the large city, where many people smile and say hello to each other on the street.

Recently, a number of studies have shown that city life is not as bad for us as we had thought, and that city dwellers on the average were as happy, if not happier(!) than small town people.

Mrs. Gold may be a little more heroic than most, but it is not at all that unusual to find the people of a building or a block or a neighborhood pulling together to fight against a common problem. And when all is said and done, life on 88th Street offers the kinds of choices that no suburb can.

See supplementary exercises on page 157.

Supplementary Exercises

SECTION ONE: HOW IT GOES TOGETHER (COHESION EXERCISES)

CHAPTER 1

The is a small but very important word in English. Here are a few ways we use it:

1. We use *the* to refer to something or someone we mentioned before.

   I saw *a man*. I said "hello" to him. *The man* did not answer.

2. We use *the* when there is only one.

   Mrs. Gold went to *the* kitchen. (There is only one kitchen.)
   Mrs. Gold walked up *the* stairs. (There is only one set of stairs that people generally use.)

3. We use *the* when we want to refer to something or someone specific.

   Mrs. Gold is sitting in her chair near *the* window. (The writers are giving us the feeling that it is a specific window and that Mrs. Gold usually sits there.)

Look at the following sentence. Find it in the story in chapter 1. Then choose the best explanation for the use of *the*.*

A truck pulls up in front of *the* building.

   a. The building was mentioned earlier in the story.
   b. There is only one building on 88th Street.
   c. This is a specific building—probably the building where Mrs. Gold lives.

Answer "a" is not correct because this is the first time the building is mentioned. Answer "b" is probably not correct—usually there are many buildings on a street. Answer "c" is the best choice.

Now, look at the following sentences. Find them in the story in chapter 1. Then choose the appropriate explanations for the use of *the*.

1. A young man gets out of *the* truck, slams the door,

Sometimes only one *answer is possible. Sometimes* two *or even all* three *are possible.*

and walks to the building.
   a. A young man gets out of the truck mentioned
      before.
   b. A young man gets out of the only truck that is on
      the street.
   c. A young man gets out of the truck that's usually in
      front of the building.
2. "A young man gets out of the truck, slams the door
   and walks to *the* building."
   a. He walks to the building that was mentioned
      before.
   b. He walks to the only building that is on 88th Street.
   c. He walks to a specific building—the one Mrs. Gold
      lives in.

CHAPTER 2

Look at the following sentences. Find them in the
dialogue in chapter 2. Then choose the appropriate
explanations for the use of *the*. Remember that more
than one explanation may be possible.
1. "*The* phone's over there."
   a. The phone that was mentioned before is over there.
   b. The only phone is over there.
   c. The specific phone—Mrs. Gold's phone—is over
      there.

2. "I was on *the* roof just now . . . ."
   a. I was on the roof that was mentioned before just
      now.
   b. I was on the roof (there is only one) just now.
   c. I was on the specific roof—the roof of this
      building—just now.
3. "Did you find *the* body?"
   a. Did you find the body of the person mentioned
      before?
   b. Did you find the only body?
   c. Did you find the specific body—the one that is
      usually on the roof?

CHAPTER 3

Look at this. Example 1:
   I met *Willie* and Mrs. Gold yesterday. I like *him* a
   lot.
Him refers to Willie.

Now look at another example. Example 2:
   I met *Willie* and *Joe* yesterday. I like *him* a lot.

Him in this case is not clear. We don't know if *him*
refers to Willie or to Joe.

In Example 1, we can say the referent is clear. It's Willie.

In Example 2, the referent is not clear. In English, you should try to make the referents very clear.

Look at the following sentences. Find them in the dialogue in chapter 3. Then choose the appropriate referents for *he, him,* and *it.*
Example: How did you know *it* was a man?
  a. How did you know Willie was a man?
  (b.) How did you know the body was a man?
  c. How did you know the thing was a man?

Now try these:
1. Is *he* dead?
  a. Is the person on the roof dead?
  b. Is Willie dead?
  c. Is Mrs. Gold dead?
2. *He* turns and speaks to Mrs. Gold.
  a. Willie turns and speaks to Mrs. Gold.
  b. Officer Walters turns and speaks to Mrs. Gold.
  c. Officer O'Neill turns and speaks to Mrs. Gold.
3. I guess *it* was about 8:00.
  a. I guess the body was about 8:00.
  b. I guess the thing was about 8:00.
  c. I guess the time was about 8:00.
4. *It's* just routine.
  a. The time is just routine.

  b. The body on the roof is just routine.
  c. Asking questions is just routine.
5. We'd appreciate *it.*
  a. We'd appreciate the body.
  b. We'd appreciate Mrs. Gold's trying to identify the body.
  c. We'd appreciate Mrs. Gold's asking some questions.

A More Difficult Exercise
Willie tells the police officers that he goes up on the roof of his building. When they ask why, he says, "I like *it.*" What does he like up there? What does *it* refer to?

CHAPTER 4
Look at the following sentences. Find them in the dialogue in chapter 4. Then choose the appropriate referents for *he, him,* and *it.*
1. Somebody typed *it* up, and I signed it.
  It refers to:
  a. the piece of paper
  b. the body on the roof
  c. everything I told them
2. Somebody typed it up, and I signed *it.*
  It refers to:
  a. the paper that they typed up

b. the police station

c. everything I told them

3. *He* had nothing but drugs.

He refers to:

a. the policeman

b. Willie

c. the kid on the roof

4. But *it* wasn't me.

It refers to:

a. some bad stuff that killed the boy on the roof

b. an overdose of drugs

c. the person who slipped him some bad stuff

A More Difficult Exercise

Mrs. Gold says, " How did *it* go last night at the police station?" What does *it* refer to?

CHAPTER 5

The pronoun *you* often refers to the listener.

Example 1:

Mrs. Gold: Good morning, Mrs. Fielding.

Mrs. Fielding: Now, isn't it about time *you* called me Anna?

In this sentence, *you* refers to Mrs. Gold.

You can be singular (as in the example above) or plural.

Example 2:

Mrs. Fielding: We've been doing a lot of thinking about the girls lately.

Mrs. Gold: What are *you* going to do?

In this sentence, *you* probably refers to Mr. and Mrs. Fielding.

We also have another use of the pronoun *you*.

Look at this example from chapter 1:

My, they're young. They look like children. I suppose that's what happens when *you* get old.

We will call this the *general you*. It does not refer to a specific person or persons. We use the *general you* when we are referring to all or most people.

Here are some more examples of the *general you*.

It's good to go to parties. *You* never know who *you'll* meet there.

You can swim in Puerto Rico all year round.

When *you* have a checking account in a bank, do they pay *you* interest?

Look at the following sentences. Find them in the dialogue in chapter 5. Then choose the appropriate referents for *you*.

1. *You* won't have long to wait.

a. Mrs. Gold
b. Mrs. Fielding
c. Willie Dorio
d. general you
e. Both a and b

2. I'd like *you* to meet Mrs. Fielding in 3W.
a. Mrs. Gold
b. Mrs. Fielding
c. Willie Dorio
d. general you
e. Both a and b

3. It makes *you* wonder.
a. Mrs. Gold
b. Mrs. Fielding
c. Willie Dorio
d. general you
e. Both b and c

4. But *you* never know.
a. Mrs. Gold
b. Mrs. Fielding
c. Willie Dorio
d. general you
e. Both a and b

5. *You* know how it is.
a. Mrs. Gold
b. Mrs. Fielding

c. Willie Dorio
d. general you
e. Both a and c

6. *You* want to give your kids something better.
a. Mrs. Gold
b. Mrs. Fielding
c. Willie Dorio
d. general you
e. Both a and b

CHAPTER 6

Look at the following sentences. Find them in the dialogue in chapter 6. Then choose the appropriate referents for *you*.

1. *You'll* have to tell me if you like it.
a. Mrs. Gold
b. Willie Dorio
c. Sally Gibson
d. general you
e. Both b and c

2. *You* can't tell from reading the recipe, you know, if it's going to be any good or not.
a. Mrs. Gold
b. Willie Dorio
c. Sally Gibson

d. general you
e. Both b and c
3. I know it, and *you* know it, but she doesn't.
   a. Mrs. Gold
   b. Willie Dorio
   c. Sally Gibson
   d. general you
   e. Both b and c
4. I'll find a way to introduce *you* two.
   a. Mrs. Gold
   b. Willie Dorio
   c. Sally Gibson
   d. general you
   e. Both b and c
5. See *you* at 8:30.
   a. Mrs. Gold
   b. Willie Dorio
   c. Sally Gibson
   d. general you
   e. Both a and c

CHAPTER 7

Look at the following sentences. Find them in the dialogue in chapter 7. Write the referent for *it, they,* and *there*.

Examples:
I'm glad to get out of *there*.
Referent: *Mrs. Gold's apartment*
It gives me a headache.
Referent: *Being polite*

1. You should try *it* more often.
   Referent: being poilte
2. Never heard of *it*.
   Referent: AThol
3. *They*'re a pain in the . . . neck.
   Referent: older sister
4. But I can tell you we don't do much Latin disco dancing *there*.
   Referent: the town of Sally Live
5. I'll bet *they*'re not like me.
   Referent: Willie's Friends

A More Difficult Exercise

1. Say *it*!
   Referent: goahead
2. But I can tell you *we* don't do much Latin disco dancing there.
   Referent: _____

CHAPTER 8

Look at these sentences. Find them in the dialogue in chapter 8. Then write the appropriate referents for the pronouns. Remember the "general you."

1. So, now *you* know the whole story.
Referent: _____

2. Whenever I go they say, "What can *you* do?"
Referent: _____

3. *You* have to be an assistant editor first.
Referent: _____

4. *They* give you tests. . . .
Referent: _____

5. They give *you* tests. . . .
Referent: _____

6. Agencies will just refer you to whatever jobs *they* have.
Referent: _____

7. Why don't *you* check it out?
Referent: _____

8. *You* can go at night.
Referent:_____

9. You can do anything *you* want to do.
Referent: _____

10. Split *it*.
Referent: _____

A More Difficult Exercise

1. Wherever I go *they* say, "What can you do?"
Referent: _____

2. Why don't you check *it* out?
Referent: _____

3. Have *it* your way.
Referent: _____

CHAPTER 9

In general, we use the word *that* to show distance from the topic of conversation in the terms of time, space, or feeling. We use *this* to refer to something present in time or space and to refer to something we feel close to. Look at the following examples from the story:

1. "How is *that* nice Cynthia Miles from church?"
(Cynthia is not present at the time the question was asked and the speaker probably doesn't know her very well.)

2. "Amanda! Enough of *that* talk."
(Anna is referring to the things that were said before. She is also indicating that she disapproves, and is therefore putting a distance between the words Amanda spoke and her own feelings.)

3. "I wish the President would do something about *this* inflation."

(The inflation that Anna is talking about is affecting her life. It is present in her mind and in her life.)

Look at the following sentences. Circle the correct word (*this/these* or *that/those*) for the given context.

1. Who's this / (that) man over there by the window?

2. Wherever did she buy this / that dress she's wearing? It's awful!

3. People have no respect for the law these / those days.

4. Operator, this / that is an emergency. Give me the police. Hurry!

5. Willie: I really feel sorry for this / that guy.

    Mrs. Gold: What guy?
    Willie: The kid on the roof.

6. Willie: I should learn to mind my own business.

    Mrs. Gold: This / That is not true, Willie.

7. In many countries they will offer you food. In the U.S. we do this, / that, too.

8. *(Mrs. Fielding is speaking to Mrs. Gold while they are standing in the hall.)*

    He lived on 89th Street in the building in the back of this / that one.

9. The funeral is this / that afternoon at this / that funeral home on Second Avenue.

10. Mrs. Fielding: I don't want our girls going to McKinley High.

    Mrs. Gold: Things are this / that bad?

11. Mrs. Gold: I'm out of sugar and flour.
    Mrs. Fielding: Let me get them for you.
    Mrs. Gold: Thank you. Let me give you some money.

    Mrs. Fielding: This / That is all right. You can pay me later. Is this / that all?

12. Later this / that evening, there is a knock on the door.

13. Who's the blond, about twenty-one, on the third floor? She lives with this / that older lady.

14. I never asked anybody to introduce me before. But I figure this / that one's different.

CHAPTER 10

Look at the following sentences. Find them in the dialogue in chapter 10. Then write the appropriate referents for *this* and *that*. Look at the following two examples:

1. Sally: Hello. Willie? *This* is Sally.
   Referent: *The person who is speaking to you on the phone now.*
2. Emily: What does he think of *that*?
   Referent: *The fact that he's a friend and that's all.*

Now try these sentences:

1. Sally: What is my type? Listen, he's a friend. *That's* all.
   Referent: _____
2. Willie: What do you mean by *that*?
   Referent: _____
3. Willie: You started me on *this*.
   Referent: _____
4. Willie: You know, I could run *that* shoe store.
   Referent: _____
5. Sally: How did you get *that* job in the first place?
   Referent: _____

CHAPTER 11

When people speak fluently, they do not always speak in complete sentences. One way to see if you understand exactly what is being said is to try to fill in the words that are missing. Look at the following examples from the dialogue in chapter 11.

Examples:

Pilar: *Mrs. Gold likes him, and so does Sally.*
Mrs. Gold likes him and Sally *likes him, too.*
Anna: *Sally's a lovely girl.*
George: She sure is.
She sure is *a lovely girl.*
Anna: Really? My Amanda is crazy about him, too.
She thinks he's "dreamy."
Pilar: *So Clara isn't the only one.*
So Clara isn't the only one *who is crazy about him.*

Now find the following sentences in the story and write in the missing words.

1. *I haven't been able to think about anything else.*
   I haven't been able to think about anything except
   _____

2. *I know what you mean.*
I know what you mean when you say that _____

_____

3. *Felipe and Consuela, our friends, left Cuba before we did.*
Felipe and Consuela, our friends, left Cuba before we

_____

4. *. . . but she couldn't tell her mother what it was.*
. . . but she couldn't tell her mother what it was that

_____

5. *He asked her what she meant.*
He asked her what she meant when she _____

_____

6. *Well, I suppose that it's true.*
Well, I suppose that it's true that _____

_____

7. *I can't say that we don't.*
I can't say that we don't _____

_____

8. *No one would have sold us one.*
No one would have sold us _____

9. *I shouldn't.*
I shouldn't _____

10. *Well, maybe a little.*
Well, maybe a little _____

_____

CHAPTER 12

Find the following sentences in the dialogue in chapter 12, and write in the words that were not spoken.

1. *Sorry. Really. I didn't know.*
Sorry. Really. I didn't know that _____

_____

2. *What's the story?*
What's the story about _____

3. *So I tell him he's dead if he tries.*
So I tell him he's dead if he tries to _____

_____

4. *So, what do you think?*
So what do you think about _____

5. *I don't know.*
I don't know _____

CHAPTER 14

Sometimes questions are a way of making a polite request.
For example:
Can you close the window? can mean the same thing as *I wish you would close the window*, or *Please close the window*.

Sometimes when you ask a question, we already know the answer.

For example:
Hey, are these (handcuffs) necessary?
Willie means that he does not think the handcuffs are necessary but knows the police think they are.

Look at the following questions made in chapter 14. Restate them in other words that say what the person really wants.
Example:
What is this?
Tell me what you want with me.
_____

1. Where do you think you're going?
_____

2. Do you have to take me in?
_____

3. (from chapter 13) Are you a Girl Scout, or something?
_____

4. (from chapter 13) Who's worrying?
_____

5. (from chapter 13) Ever heard of perjury?
_____

CHAPTER 15

In chapter 15, a few words are used over and over again in the conversation. Some of these words are:
perjury
lawyer
cookie

1. In thinking back over the entire book, what words appear over and over again? Get together with two or three classmates and make a list of them.
2. Which of the words you listed above tell the main ideas of the book? List them here.

SECTION 2: HOW IT'S USED
(GRAMMAR EXERCISES)

CHAPTER 1

A. Interjections

"Oh," she moans, "I'm getting old."

In the sentence above, "Oh" is an *interjection*.
Interjections can be sounds that people make to show
their feelings of surprise, happiness, sadness, etc. Here
are some interjections and their meanings.

Hmmm . . .	(the person is thinking)
Huh?	(the person is surprised)
Oops!	(the person has done something wrong)
Uh-oh	(the person believes there is going to be trouble)
Ow!	(the person is hurt)

Find two more interjections in the story. Write them
here:

1. Oh
2.
3.

B. Choose the Correct Form

Circle the correct forms. Don't look at the original story.

closes
1. Her eyes open and closing as she rests.
(close)

looks
2. Some noise makes her open her eyes and looking out
look
at 88th Street.

slams
3. A young man gets out of the truck, slamming the
slam
walks
door, and walking to the building.
walk

keeps
4. I'd better go and keeping an eye on things.
keep

Now try these sentences:

comes
1. The first young man coming down the stairs and
come
goes
going outside.
go

	opens		begins
2.	Together they opening the back and beginning taking		
	open		begin

out some chairs, table, and a bed.

	closes		goes
3.	She closing her eyes and going to sleep.		
	close		go

You will notice when you finish this exercise that when one subject has two main verbs following it, the verbs are usually in the same form.

He gets up and opens the door.
This is called parallel construction.

CHAPTER 2

A. Had better

Look at this sentence from the story:
"I'*d better* use your phone now."

I'd better = I had better

We often use *had better* when we are making a suggestion or making a choice.

Look at the following examples:

a. Did you hear that? It sounded like a gun. You'*d better* call the police.

b. Takashi has a test tomorrow. He'*d better* study.

c. I'm getting a little fat. I'*d better* stop eating bread.

In this exercise, read the problems and look at some possible solutions. Select the best one (in your opinion) and use it in a sentence with *had better*. (You can write your own advice if you don't like any of the ones suggested.)

Example:

Problem: It's nine o'clock at night. A lady is coming home late from work. She hears a man's footsteps behind her. There is no one else around. What should she do?

Possibilities: call for help
run for her apartment
walk faster
go over to the other side of the street
turn around and hit the man

Advice: She'*d better* go over to the other side of the street and see if he follows.

Now try these problems:

1. Problem: Carmen wakes up at 2:00 in the morning. Her neighbors, Mr. and Mrs. Green, are shouting at each other. Mr. Green shouts

that he's going to kill Mrs. Green. What
should Carmen do?

Possibilities: call the police
ring the Green's doorbell
shout at the Greens to be quiet
forget it and go back to sleep

Advice: _____

_____

2. Problem: Ono is reading a book in the living room.
He smells smoke. He goes to the kitchen
and sees the room is full of smoke.

Possibilities: leave his apartment and knock on all the
neighbors' doors
call the fire department and then leave his
apartment
collect his most valuable possessions and
then leave
knock on all the doors of his neighbors and
then go back for his most valuable
possessions
leave his apartment and call the fire
department from a pay phone
open all the windows

Advice: _____

_____

Should *and* ought to *are often synonyms for* had better.

B. Choose the Correct Form (Parallel construction)

1. I was on the roof just now and I ~~see~~ (saw) this dark shape
sees
in the corner.

2. Mrs. Gold gets up and went to the door.
go / goes

Now do these sentences:

1. I went nearer and saw it was a person.
go / goes   see / sees

2. She pressed the buzzer and spoke through the
intercom.
press / presses   speak / speaks

CHAPTER 3 Unshifted Questions

Look at this piece of dialogue from the story:

O'Neill: Your address?
Willie: 229 88th Street. Apartment 5W.
O'Neill: *You don't live in this apartment?*

Look at the difference between these two questions:

You don't live here?
Don't you live here?

Sometimes, in conversation, to show surprise, we use the word order of a statement instead of a question. Our voices go up at the end of both questions. The intonation of these two questions is the same. Say them to yourself.

Do you think I don't know how old I am?
You think I don't know how old I am?

Now look at these examples:

1. Mrs. Gold: Hello, Willie.
   Willie: Can I use your phone?
   Mrs. Gold: *You don't have one yet?*
2. Willie: I want to report a body on our roof.
   Mrs. Gold: *There's a body on our roof?*

In the following exercise, see if you can write a question to show surprise. Use the word order of a statement.

1. Willie: I don't feel well.

Mrs. Gold: Are you going to work?
Willie: No.
Mrs. Gold: _____ ?
2. Mrs. Gold: Come in, Willie.
   Willie: Do you have any cake today?
   Mrs. Gold: I didn't make any.
   Willie: _____ ?
3. Willie: Did you see the accident?
   Mrs. Gold: What accident?
   Willie: _____ ?

A More Difficult Exercise

Add something new or change your response a little.

Example:
Willie: Officer Walters is married and has five girls and two boys.
Mrs. Gold: *Officer Walters has seven children?*

Now try this:
Willie: I live alone.
Mrs. Gold: _____ ?

CHAPTER 4 Reported Speech

Look at this example:

Detective: *(to Willie)* What did you see? What did you do?

Later that night
Willie: *(to Mrs. Gold)* I told them what I saw and did.*

When the main verb is past in reported speech, very often (but not always) the verbs that follow will be in the past form.

I *told* them what I *saw* and *did*.

Notice also that the verbs are unshifted (they are not in their question position or question form.)

Look at one more example:
Detective: *(to Mrs. Gold)* What kind of people go in and out of his apartment?
Later that night
Mrs. Gold: *(to Willie)* They wanted to know what kind of people went in and out of your apartment.

Now try the following exercise:
1. Detective: *(to Mrs. Gold)* Does he know anyone from the neighborhood?

Later that day
Mrs. Gold: *(to Willie)*   They wanted to know if you

_____

2. Detective: *(to Mrs. Gold)* Does he know the dead boy?
Later that day
Mrs. Gold: *(to Willie)*   They wanted to know if ____

3. Detective: *(to Mrs. Gold)* Does he act strangely?
Later that day
Mrs. Gold: *(to Willie)*   They wanted to know if ____

_____

4. Mrs. Gold: *(to Willie)*   Did you see a needle up there?

Willie: *(to Mrs. Gold)*   The police asked me if ____

_____

A More Difficult Exercise

5. Mrs. Gold: *(to the detectives)* He's a nice young man.
Later that day
Mrs. Gold: *(to Willie)*   I told them what ____

_____

In formal English, to report a statement said in the simple past tense, the verbs that follow the main verb would be in the past perfect: I told them what I had seen *and* done.

CHAPTER 7 Exclamations

In this chapter, Willie says:

Boy, am I glad to get out of there.

This is *not* a question. (The position of the subject and the verb make it look like a question, but it isn't). Instead, Willie is using a "question pattern" to show he is saying something with a lot of feeling.
Here are some more examples:

1. Willie: Am I making a lot of noise?

    George: Are you making a lot of noise!

In this example, George uses a "question pattern" to make fun of Willie's foolish question.

2. Boy am I hungry.
3. Man, is he tall.

Notice, as in the two examples above, this pattern has a word or phrase in front of it. These words or phrases indicate feeling. Below are a few of the milder words and phrases.

Boy

Man

These are used with positive and negative statements.

Brother

This is used only with negative statements.

As in all languages, there are stronger words in English, too. You can learn them by listening to Americans. Change the following sentences into exclamations.

Example: You feel very angry.

Brother, am I angry!

1. You hate paying taxes.
2. You went to a terrible movie.
3. You love chocolate cake.
4. Your car is driving you crazy.
5. You hate the winter.

CHAPTER 9 *What* and *What For?*

Look at these sentences from chapter 9.

Where?

What for?

What about your job?

What for in this example means the same as "why." *What for,* when the two words come together, is a complete sentence. You cannot begin a sentence with *what for*. You can, however, begin your sentence with *what* and end the sentence with *for* (see Example 2).

Look at the examples.

1. *Why* are you studying so hard?

2. *What* are you studying so hard *for*?

Now look at these sentences. Question the speaker of these sentences.
Use what . . . for?
 Example:
 She's learning to write with both hands. *What's she* _____
 learning to do that for? _____

1. He gave all his money to his sister. _____
_____ ?

2. I have to watch a TV program at 6:00 A.M. tomorrow morning. _____
_____ ?

3. He bought a $500.00 suit. _____ ?
4. She cut off her beautiful long hair. _____
_____ ?

CHAPTER 11 Otherwise

Look at this sentence from chapter 11.
 They'll help you out if you're in trouble, but, otherwise, they want to be left alone.
Otherwise, here, stands for the clause *if you are not in trouble.* Now look at another example:
 If my meeting ends early, I'll be home early.
 Otherwise, I'll be home at the regular time.

In the sentence above, *otherwise* stands for:
 If my meeting doesn't end early,

Here is another example:
 If you don't feel well, I'll stay with you. Otherwise, I'll go home.
In the sentence above, *otherwise* stands for:
 If you feel well,

For each of these sentences, write a sentence that begins with *otherwise.* Use your own ideas in writing your sentences.
 Example:
 If you are hungry, I'll start dinner now. *Otherwise, I'll finish my homework.*

1. If you understand this work, we can go on to the next chapter. _____
_____

2. He has to save his money if he wants to go to Europe this summer. _____
_____

3. I've got to finish my homework this afternoon. _____
_____

4. I think you should take a taxi. _____
_____

5. I hope the weather is good. _____